AF333858

"The LifeCycle is an ingenious approach to creating a new life. Taking small steps consistently, as the LifeCycle encourages, does lead to big changes."

— Monica in Los Angeles, California

"I'll never look at relationships the same way again. Your comments about 'what we put in front' vs 'what we keep in back' has given me the freedom to see what is deep and true in a person."

— Betsy in Sarasota, Florida

"Being an architect who matches living spaces with the needs of people...when all the parts of a plan come together as a whole, you generally have a great design. Your 'design' is a plan for life."

— Paul in San Diego, California

"A simple, straightforward, yet powerful method for increasing personal power, understanding and self-fulfillment."

— Blanche in Chicago, Illinois

"I had been thinking about exercising and taking vitamins, and when I picked up this book to read, that was the push I needed."

— Katie in Nashville, Tennessee

"I felt as if the book was speaking to me...ways I would think and paths so easily seen that I breathe easier and smile more."

— Jeannie in Sumner, Washington

LifeCycle

Holism and Evolution
The original source of the holistic
approach to life

LifeCycle

You <u>can</u> have what you want most.

Sanford Holst

Sierra Sunrise Books

Sierra Sunrise Publishing
14622 Ventura Boulevard, PMB 800
Sherman Oaks, California 91403

First Printing: October, 1999

Publisher's Cataloging-in-Publication Data

Holst, Sanford.
        Lifecycle : you can have what you want most /
Sanford Holst.
        -- 1st ed.
        p. cm.
        Life cycle
        Includes bibliographical references and index.
        LCCN: 99-71158
        ISBN: 1-887263-12-8

        1. Self-actualization (Psychology) 2. Success.
        3. Psychology, Applied.   I. Title. II. Title:
        Life cycle

        F637.S4H65 1999   158.1
                                           QBI99-671

Table of Contents

A Better Life

Have you ever felt your life could be much better than it is today?

Most of us have thought that. Yet something seems to hold us back—as though there were some secrets we need to know, but no one's told us. Some people must know the answers, because they're wildly successful—while we struggle.

It turns out there *are* some secrets. Or at the very least, some things which are rarely told and even less often put into practice. You're about to discover them— and how to use them in a way that can produce dramatic improvements in your life.

How do you know these "secrets" are the real thing? Because they've already helped other people from all walks of life. But even more important...you will soon see how they work in your own life.

A woman in her early thirties named Elaine sat down at my table one night in our neighborhood coffeehouse. The locals know I have a collection of facts on health from writing about it for many years. Elaine wondered if I could help her with a health problem.

I said I wasn't a medical practitioner, but encouraged her to talk about what was bothering her.

It turned out she had a range of problems including sleeplessness, skin problems and migraines. This made it difficult to perform the long hours of work required by her demanding boss. Especially since she had to rush home from work each day to see her children and make dinner for her husband—who was growing more distant and irritable. Spending quality time with her kids was impossible, let alone finding time for herself.

She was at her wits' end. Her health seemed to be spiraling downward, even though she was taking prescription medicine, vitamins and herbs.

I finally got the picture. Elaine had a health problem. But even more important, she had a problem with her life.

I tried to show her how the different parts of her life were tied together—what's known as the holistic view of life. Her work seemed to be affecting her health. Relationship problems were affecting her health. Anxiety was affecting her health. All her resulting health problems seemed to be aggravating her work, relationships, and everything else.

She asked anxiously, "What can I *do*? It's so overwhelming."

"Don't tackle everything at once," I suggested. "Pick one small thing to make your situation better. Start with something that has nothing to do with your health. And do it. Then call me and we'll talk again."

A few days later, Elaine called. She had told her boss some "problems at home" required she no longer work overtime. She was nervous, but excited. Now she could do more things for the kids and her husband.

"That's great," I acknowledged. "But first do something for yourself."

She seemed surprised. I explained that unless she was physically and emotionally OK, she wouldn't be able to help the other family members very much.

She settled on a cup of tea for herself in a quiet place where she could read. She would do it for twenty minutes each day before starting dinner. Once she got that in place, she could pick something to help her family.

A month later, she called to say most of her health problems had miraculously cleared up. And her home life had improved. She seemed to be bursting with energy. Some things were still rocky, and she still had more projects to do. But she seemed to be enjoying her life much more than before.

I could feel her happiness. And I'll tell you, helping make that happen has got to be one of the greatest feelings there is!

My experience with Elaine was the first glimpse I had of what things were possible. It's grown tremendously since then.

Like a new plant poking its head above the soil to greet the sunlight, the basic methods shown here are quickly mastered and produce their first results right away. It's only a beginning, of course. Like that small plant, the steps you take will continue to grow and can bear fruit for many years.

One of the keys to this rapid growth is to recognize—and use to your advantage—the several different parts of your life.

When you were growing up, you learned new things all the time—but my guess is no one ever showed you the whole picture: what all the parts of your life are, how they work, and how they can come together to give you a better...even a *great*...life.

That's how I grew up too. Then by some fortunate combination of hard work and good luck, the right pieces came together and I found the LifeCycle. It's a process that helps you develop a healthy body, great relationships, a successful career, enjoyable surroundings and peace of mind. And helps you use all of them together to accomplish almost anything you want.

It can be a real breakthrough in your life.

What do these breakthroughs feel like? That's hard to explain. Instead let me share a related experience with you.

After graduating from high school in Flagstaff, Arizona, I got a job working as a ranger for the U. S. Forest Service. Driving a battered, green pickup truck with fire-fighting tools in back, I traveled dirt roads among the mountains and forests near the Grand Canyon looking for fires.

To understand what this meant to an impressionable young man, you'd have to know that my father was a career Army officer and strict discipline governed our home. We called him, "Sir." Punishments were doled out with a leather belt. As a kid I escaped to school or Boy Scouts to get away. I never knew where I was going, just away.

Now here I was, driving back mountain roads and walking dusty trails in boots and khaki outfit with a Forest Service badge hanging from my shirt pocket. I watched for smoke and counseled campers about their fires. I was doing the same job as men in their thirties and forties. And loving it.

Whenever a call came over the two-way radio about a new forest fire, my pickup truck was always among the first to arrive. As the truck skidded to a stop I'd jump out, grab tools and run for the fire. It was hot, sweaty, smokey work. We worked side-by-side to dig fire-breaks around the flaming trees, trying to contain the fire before it spread. At night we collapsed beside a campfire, ate something, drank sooty coffee, and went to sleep under the brightest stars you ever saw in your life.

It was one of those magical times you want to go on forever.

It was a life-changing experience, a real breakthrough, though at the time I didn't know why.

It had to do with breaking free from things that were holding me back. I began to have a life of my own. I knew what I wanted to do and went after it. There was a college degree in my future. Two of them, in fact.

It was a step forward that happened by chance.

Now I've learned why it happened, and how to make my life go forward by choice.

I'd like to share that discovery with you. It can bring something exciting and new into your life!

What Would You Like to Have?

Before we explore the insights, understandings and steps that will help you move your life forward, there's an important step that needs to be taken. You need to know where you're going.

You may already have a clear idea of something that's holding you back, or something you want to have. That's great. Keep it in mind. But one of the things that happens to most of us is we take a very short-sighted view of life. It's only natural. Our problems are today, our energies seem so limited, we just plow ahead on whatever course seems most important. Then we win or lose on that path, stop, look around, and take off in some other direction. This process is described in scientific circles by the colorful name "drunkard's walk." We tend to zig-zag a lot. And sometimes end up back where we started. Let's take a moment now to look ahead and see where you want to go.

The best way to start is to mark your choices on the following questionnaire. It identifies good things you might like to have in your life. There are no right or wrong answers, they're different for everyone. The results are just for you.

This whole journey you're starting is about your life, and how it can keep getting better. To do that, you need to actually participate. Write down anything and everything that will help you. Later, if you don't want to keep something you can mark it out. But I think you'll find the notes you make here are a valuable lodestar, a compass you can refer to again and again to keep your life on track—and maybe see how much you've grown and adapted to a better life.

Important!

Write your answers in this book.
The LifeCycle is an interactive process.
If you're "just looking" you
won't achieve what you want.
If you participate, you'll get everything there is.

Many of the things people have said they want in their life are shown under the following headings, though you probably could add some more. Which ones do it for you?

MARK ONES YOU'D LIKE TO HAVE

Health

Good enough to enjoy life	☐
Athletic competitor and winner	☐
Overcome a problem	☐

Money

Have a little more than now	☐
Really wealthy	☐
Need enough for retirement	☐

Relationships

Have more relationships	☐
Get someone really great for you	☐
Solve current relationship problem	☐

Security

Be less worried	☐
Feel much safer	☐
Deal with anxiety, depression	☐

Respect and Appreciation

Want a little more of it	☐
Would like to be famous	☐
Overcome some disrespect	☐

Success

Want your fair share of it	☐
Reach the very top	☐
Recover from a past problem	☐

Leadership

Enjoy having more people around you	☐
Many people follow the direction you go	☐
Escape a demanding person	☐

Things

Better personal belongings	☐
Beautiful home and property	☐
Replace something that's run-down	☐

Activities

Sports you really enjoy	☐
Vacations to fantastic places	☐
Overcome something that limits you	☐

Friends

People you like to be with	☐
Friends who help make your life better	☐
New, fascinating people interested in you	☐

Take another look at the things you marked above and pick out a few which mean the most to you. Which ones are highest on your list? Which give you the greatest feeling of, "Yes, I want that!" Copy them here, and maybe add some specific details or examples after each.

❍ ______________________________

❍ ______________________________

❍ ______________________________

❍ ______________________________

❍ ______________________________

That's a very good start. Clearly visualizing what you want is the first step to getting it.

Take a minute to re-read the things you wrote on these lines. Imagine how it would feel to have those good things in your life.

Now consider this. Those things are real. Other people have them. You can have them. Soon you'll see how you can bring them into your life.

The LifeCycle

You have many resources available to build a better life—probably more than you realize. We're about to explore them.

To really understand the LifeCycle, it helps to know where it came from. Similar to the headwaters of a river, the source goes back to small streams in the hills of recorded history.

Like one of the adventurers in the Greek epics *Iliad* and *Odyssey* who journeyed to strange lands and brought back things of value for their people, I've had the good fortune to make some amazing discoveries.

The first of these is that things haven't changed much in thousands of years. The Hindu *Vedas* and the Chinese *I Ching* deal with life choices—the basic material from which most movies and dramas are made.

Socrates' **Dialogues** (*written down by Plato*) sounds like dinner table conversation anywhere in the world today. It turns out Socrates was a very worldly fellow who made a living by engaging wealthy people in spirited conversations about life, and earned sponsorship by those patrons.

In many ways, he personified the characteristics of a full life as it's now defined in the LifeCycle. His health was excellent right up to his seventieth birthday. His career was of the super-star category. You can mention his name today and everyone knows who he is. His mastery of personal relationships was outstanding—he was able to maintain very comfortable surroundings based on having conversations. Due to the politics of the day he had to drink hemlock, but that's another story. He had great peace of mind, amply illustrated in the spirited and cheerful demeanor with which he always presented himself.

Without going too far afield into ancient things you may not be interested in, let me just mention that Lao Tzu, Confucius, Gautama Buddha and many others through the ages also made significant contributions to our understanding of life and the world around us. More recently, I would add Jan Christiaan Smuts who gave us the holistic view of the world, and Deepak Chopra whose remarkable contributions still continue.

The world's religions, both Western and Eastern, have had a profound effect on our feelings about what constitutes a good life, and are a strong influence today on how people see things and what they do.

Added to this are a rainbow of different approaches to self-awareness, nutrition, relationships, twelve-step programs, life-building seminars, coping workshops and similar positive efforts.

Some intense programs are not planned, but given to us by life—like the experience I had in the Forest Service. It broke the tight mold that held me, and let all these other ways of looking at life find their way in.

As a result, I've participated in many of these religious and development groups, and found each to have its own particular value, focus and thoughts.

Yet even after experiencing these wonderful creations from many sources, I was still seeking something. Down deep, I felt there had to be something very basic which tied together all these ideas about life and its different parts—something that would help it all make sense.

One day in 1998 I was in my writing room facing out through French doors to the fruit trees, grass and flowers in the back yard. Sunlight streamed down. It was a comfortable 1st of March in Los Angeles. Propped open in front of me was a copy of ***Holism and Evolution***, the remarkable book that started the holistic approach to life. Finding this book had been a discovery in itself. I had always thought the holistic concept went back a long time, probably to vague sources in Asia—but had never gotten around to pursuing it. Once I got on that trail I was surprised to discover the entire concept sprang from this single book published in 1926 by Jan Christiaan Smuts. The thing I couldn't figure out was why, since the essential holistic principle says everything in the universe is made up of wholes, it was mainly applied to holistic health today and very little else.

Pondering this strange turn of events, I looked up from the book and gazed at the bright colors in the yard. It was a particularly relaxing early-Spring morning. I asked myself, "What is a whole, full life?"

The answer came back almost immediately.

It was simple and clear. I was stunned that I hadn't seen it before.

The answer was that five things, taken together, give us a complete and satisfying life:

- ○ Healthy Body
- ○ Great Relationships
- ○ Successful Career
- ○ Enjoyable Surroundings
- ○ Peace of Mind.

With that, the ideas, beliefs, facts and teachings from hundreds of different sources began falling into place.

A diagram came to mind. I quickly sketched it on a piece of paper. Insights and words began to flow effortlessly. The pad of paper filled up quickly. I started another. All day I wrote, finally falling into bed about three in the morning.

In the months that followed, I gave this diagram and a short write-up to many people and asked what they thought. Almost everyone had their own insight.

The idea of a LifeCycle *process* took root and grew, providing a way to put the concept to use in every-day life. More people tried it, and the feedback was amazing.

Now I'm showing this to you so you can share those insights and benefits as well.

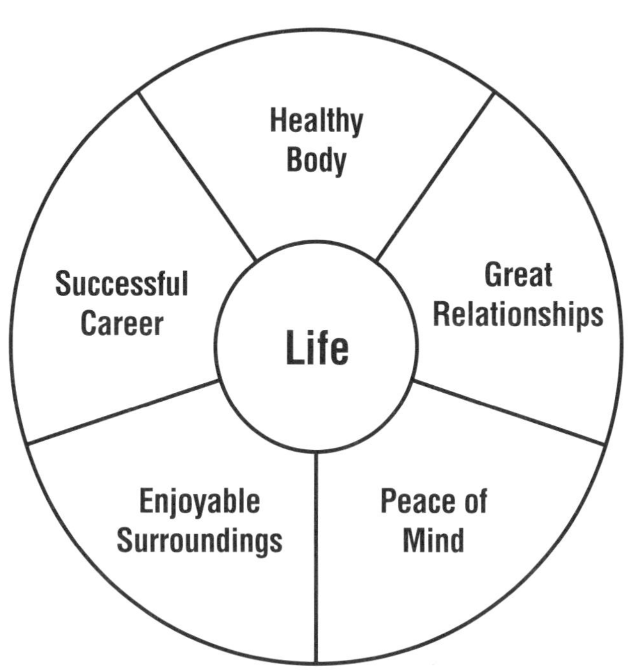

LifeCycle

> *To live is like to love —*
> *all reason is against it,*
> *and all healthy instinct for it.*
>
> *— Samuel Butler*

Life

For most of us, the world seems filled with millions of small things we have to know or do—and if we don't know or do them, we get tripped up. Other people get the attractive person we wanted. Other people get the job we wanted. Other people get into great shape easily. The list goes on and on. What are all those things we need to know? How can those good things happen to us?

Most people are relieved to discover there are only five basic parts to their life. And good things start to happen when they take a series of small steps in these areas.

Let's take a brief look at each of these parts of your life.

Healthy Body

I'm sure you're very aware how important your body is to your life.

On days when you feel strong, healthy and full of energy, it seems there isn't anything you can't do.

But some people don't take care of their body and their health spirals downward—even to the point of a pre-mature death in some cases. Short of that, they may develop disabilities or serious illnesses which restrict their ability to lead a normal life. Most people are better off than that, but in not-very-good shape...they're able to do daily tasks but without much energy and are confined to bed several times a year due to sickness. Smaller numbers of people work on their health and manage to stay fit and active. A few become outstanding athletes able to earn a living or win prestigious awards due to their physical prowess.

What we're talking about now is moving up that scale...taking your life out of danger, being less susceptible to illness, having more energy and enjoying robust, good health.

Beauty and physical attractiveness are included here, as well as sexual potency. Those come together as you achieve a vibrant state of health. Better vision, hearing, sense of smell, taste and touch are also included.

Almost all of us have something about our physical body that isn't perfect. That's OK. There are ways to improve what you have, and ways to work around it to move far ahead of where most people are today.

Great Relationships

Relationships are another vital part of your life. Much of what you do is done with other people—or strongly affected by what others do. Even simple enjoyment of life is often linked to enjoying it with someone else.

We all grew up with experiences that shape our ability to create and build relationships. Some of us feel under attack by others all the time. Others tend to be reclusive, staying by themselves and disliking upsets caused by unwanted intrusions. Some have a small circle of friends. Others have larger circles and make new friends to replace those who drift away. A few, special people seem to make more friends wherever they go, always getting invitations and special favors.

Regardless of where you may be in this spectrum today, a few basic concepts allow you to relax and build relationships easily and naturally.

The relationship is included in this area—the special person you marry, and who may have children with you. The one with whom you may share the rest of your life.

This also includes pets, family relationships, business relationships, and even relationships with groups of people.

The experiences which shaped your ability to have or not have good relationships are in the past. The ability to go forward and have great relationships is in your future. And it doesn't have to be the distant future.

Successful Career

Everyone has a career, even if they're not entirely aware of it. This may be the traditional "been doing it for ten years and plan to do it until I retire" career. Or it may be something you do for a while before going on to something else. Changing careers in the middle of your life is not uncommon any more.

Not all careers are paid, but they're careers just the same. Almost all of us started with the career of "student" and did it steadily for twelve years or more. Homemaker is another career which usually spans many years, involves a lot of work and contributes significantly to the success of family members.

Also, people can have more than one career at a time. Some hobbies become careers. They go on for years and build your reputation as an expert in some area. Even the avid pursuit of a sport can be a career—whether you play professionally or compete for weekend bragging rights.

A career might be a job you don't like, but you're stuck in it because it seems to be the only way you can earn money. Or it may be a job you don't mind doing but aren't really interested in—the best parts being payday and getting free at 5:00. Or it can be work in a field you enjoy, but your career growth and pay increases are as slow as molasses. Or you're doing well, but other people are doing better and getting the lucky breaks. Or you can be sitting on top of your field, widely respected, highly paid, and able to call your own shots.

At the moment, you may be in any one of these situations. If you want to move up, you can.

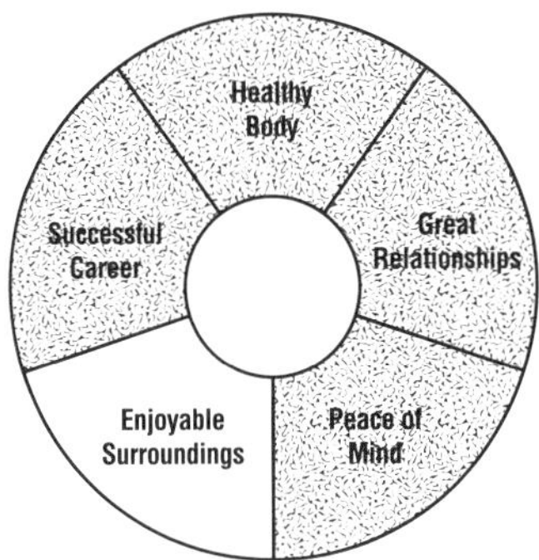

Enjoyable Surroundings

The things around you are an important part of your life. In fact, many people measure their life in terms of the things they have. The car. The house. The jewelry.

There's nothing wrong with having those things. In a better world, everyone would have them.

But your surroundings are also much more. It's the trees and flowers in your neighborhood—or lack of them. It's the blue sky and sunshine above you. It's the condition of rooms you live in, the condition of the place where you work.

Some people live in tenements with holes in the walls, roaches in the kitchen, no hot water, graffiti on neighboring buildings—and go to work in a place which is more of the same. Others share a cheap apartment, drive a beat-up car and work for minimum wage. More people have an OK place to live, an average job in an average place, and take vacation trips to places like Disneyland. Some have a house with a yard, get a new car every few years, wear good clothes, work in a nice office and take vacation trips to Hawaii or Bermuda. A smaller number live on estates, have three new cars, work in an over-sized office with expensive furniture, and take vacations in places most of us have only seen in magazines.

It's yours if you want it enough.

Peace of Mind

Although often over-looked, this is a key part of your life. Worries can keep you from enjoying what would otherwise be a great life. Small fears sit in the back of most people's minds, brought out by things like walking through a poorly-lit city neighborhood at night.

From time to time, almost everyone has some nagging doubts. Did I do too much of that...did I do too little? I wish I hadn't said that...are they offended? Sometimes, unpleasant experiences and critical voices we heard in the past still lurk in the back of our mind. Not smart enough. Not brave enough. Not attractive enough. On and on.

Some people have so many worries, fears and doubts they become paralyzed and unable to function—

stuck in their home and afraid to come out. Others have a very limited life, not looking at people unless they have to, and having few friends. Many people are able to suppress worries and doubts, yet still find themselves going over disturbing things again and again. Others are able to deal with things as they come up, then let them go—and are less likely to get upset. A few seem happy with their lot in life, unflappable and upbeat, with a natural, ready smile. That's a good place to be.

If you want, you can free yourself from the "baggage" that weighs on you and really enjoy all the good things in your life.

Cycle

Many cycles flow through your life, making it richer and making change and growth possible. Let's look at a few of them, and see how they can help you get what you want and need in life.

About once every second your body goes through a "heartbeat" cycle which opens and closes valves, squeezes heart muscles and sends blood coursing throughout your body. It energizes and sustains you. This cycle is repeated about seventy times a minute.

Each day is also a cycle happening around you and inside you. Outside, night gives way to day, birds start looking for food, traffic picks up on the streets, towns and cities come alive with activity...then night falls, towns and cities quiet down, traffic ebbs, birds nest for the night and things become quiet under the stars. Inside, you wake up, do a morning routine of washing, dressing and eating, then start doing your work of the day (*earning money or otherwise keeping your life moving forward*), with evenings usually given over to relaxation, then going to sleep for the night. This cycle is repeated about 365 times a year.

Each year in your life is a cycle, around you and inside you. The warmth of summer, colored leaves of fall, coldness of winter and blooming flowers of spring are familiar signs of this passage. Each year also marks an important cycle in your life. I'm sure you remember the school year cycle when you were growing up...the anticipation of moving up a grade in the fall, the confusion of new classes, the grind of homework and tests, the victories and setbacks of grades, the exhilaration of being *done* and away for the summer.

Was each annual cycle important? Do you remember when the people in the grade above you seemed so old and worldly...and kids in the grade below seemed so young and childish? After you leave school the annual cycle rolls on, even if not as clearly drawn. It's still marked by anxiety-producing annual reviews at work and celebratory annual salary increases, as well as birthdays, holidays, and another notch on most measuring sticks (*resident for 'x' years, more benefits at 'y' years*). This cycle is repeated about seventy-five times in each life.

Life and growth are dependent on cycles.

Going with the flow of our life, the LifeCycle process begins with a better understanding of where we are and where we want to be. It recognizes that to achieve our life's goals in one giant leap is usually just not possible physically, mentally or emotionally—and those who try almost always end in failure.

Instead, consistent with the flow of life, a small step forward is made in each improvement cycle. Then the cycle is repeated, and repeated again. Almost before you know it, these small steps have added up to a major change in your life. The achievement of your life's goals, as well as the happiness and satisfaction of having a great life, are waiting for you.

Connections

Up to this point we've looked at the five parts of your life as if they were separate from each other. Actually, there are many connections between them and cycles flow back and forth through them.

A simple statement sums up these connections:

As you improve one part of your life, all the other parts improve. By improving all the parts, your whole life becomes better.

Let's look at an example of how this works.

Having a healthy body contributes strongly to giving you a full and satisfying life. It also produces fewer physical failures and worries, and in that way contributes to your peace of mind. A healthy body is attractive to others, making it easier to develop good relationships, particularly of a sexual nature. A healthy body also contributes to a successful career, allowing you to participate in all the work and activities needed to be successful. And a healthy body allows you to create an enjoyable environment, maintain the things you own, and gather around you things you find pleasing and satisfying.

In the same way, each of the other parts of your life contributes strongly to the rest. Improving any one of them causes a cycle of improvement to flow through all of them.

Learning to see yourself as a whole person can help you create a richer and more satisfying life.

Your Starting Place

All of us grow up with different experiences. We all have different sets of strengths and needs in our life. Fortunately, you can customize the LifeCycle steps so they're appropriate to your own life.

Many people have asked for an indicator to show their starting place, so I created the following questionnaire.

It shows you the relative strengths which currently exist in each of the five parts of your life. Knowing that, it's easier for you to take advantage of those strengths and identify the steps which help improve your life.

You don't need to be concerned about getting a lower score than someone else. The answers are balanced so everyone's total is the same. (*I wish people had done that when I was in school.*) Instead, you get a measure of which areas are stronger in your life today. That in turn gives you a leg up on the path to building a better and happier life.

Suggestion: don't try to "figure out" the questionnaire—just have fun with it.

Where You Are Today

Each line in the following list has two choices. Consider which one has more to do with your life *today* and mark the box next to it. If both choices do not seem highly relevant to you, pick whichever is more relevant than the other.

There is no right or wrong answer on these. Go with your first impression on each of them—that always gives the best results.

Try to pick a box on the left or right each time. Only mark the box in the middle if you really can't say one applies more to your life than the other. Mark one box on each line.

	A	**B**	**C**	
1. You are popular	☐	☐	☐	You are in shape
2. Your things need repair	☐	☐	☐	You are worried
3. You often have organic food	☐	☐	☐	You are a supervisor
4. You are anxious	☐	☐	☐	You are shy
5. You are well-paid	☐	☐	☐	You see much greenery

	A	B	C	
6. You are tired	☐	☐	☐	You see much graffiti
7. Your things are new	☐	☐	☐	You are relaxed
8. Your things are cheap	☐	☐	☐	You have enemies
9. You are calm	☐	☐	☐	You are invited
10. A glass-ceiling is above you	☐	☐	☐	You are depressed
11. You have bonuses	☐	☐	☐	You have friends
12. You are often concerned	☐	☐	☐	You often use medicine
13. You go to parties	☐	☐	☐	Your things are well-kept
14. You are a loner	☐	☐	☐	You have illnesses
15. You are energetic	☐	☐	☐	Your things are soothing
16. You are underpaid	☐	☐	☐	Your things are dirty
17. You feel reassured	☐	☐	☐	You often use vitamins
18. You often have fast-food	☐	☐	☐	You are supervised
19. Your things are expensive	☐	☐	☐	You get advancement
20. You are solemn	☐	☐	☐	You are overworked

That wasn't so hard, was it? I've been told the choices offered are a little strange, but it does work.

Now, go over the results and see what you get. For example, in the Health group below, "1C" means: if the third box on line 1 (*Box 1C*) has a mark in it, fill in a circle under the Health group. If not, don't fill in a circle. Then go on to Box 3A, and so on.

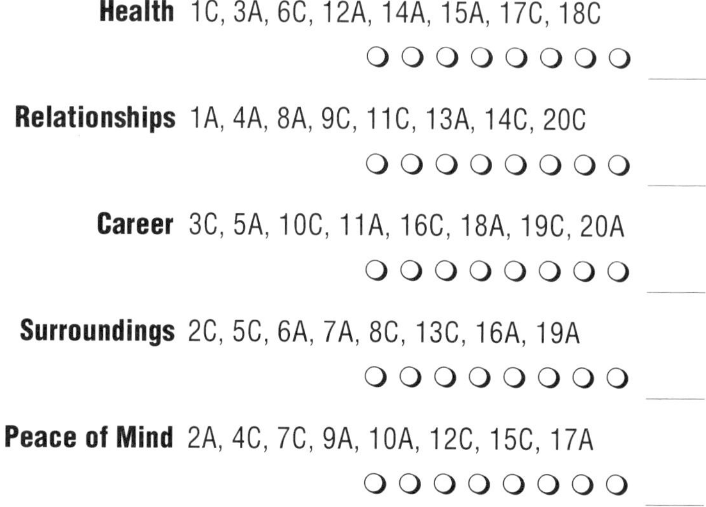

Health   1C, 3A, 6C, 12A, 14A, 15A, 17C, 18C

O O O O O O O O   _____

Relationships   1A, 4A, 8A, 9C, 11C, 13A, 14C, 20C

O O O O O O O O   _____

Career   3C, 5A, 10C, 11A, 16C, 18A, 19C, 20A

O O O O O O O O   _____

Surroundings   2C, 5C, 6A, 7A, 8C, 13C, 16A, 19A

O O O O O O O O   _____

Peace of Mind   2A, 4C, 7C, 9A, 10A, 12C, 15C, 17A

O O O O O O O O   _____

After you've gone through all of the boxes, count up the number of filled-in circles in each group. Write that number on the line following the circles.

This is what the results mean: the highest numbers are the areas where you seem to have the greatest strengths at this point. The remaining items are where you can make the fastest progress, since they are not yet up with the other areas.

If you happen to end up with all the numbers being about the same (*all are 3-4*) that's actually a good starting place too. It means all the areas are about the same for you, so you can pick any of the five in terms of where to start adding to your life.

LifeCycle Connections

In recent years the mind-body connection has been seen to produce a strong, positive effect on our health. Deepak Chopra, Bernie Siegel and many others have shown us how to take advantage of this connection, and have provided insights on how to improve our lives.

And yet...mind-body is only one of many connections in your life. While this may seem surprising at first, once you see the connections it makes complete sense.

The effect of these many connections is so strong that if you're not aware of them and let them deteriorate, you may find yourself caught in a downward spiral. Problems in one area drag down all the others.

But the opposite is also true. If you're aware of the connections, you can use them to your benefit. You can create an upward spiral that takes you to a healthy, prosperous and rewarding life.

There are a total of ten connections between the different parts of your life. And each plays an important role.

Mind - Body

Your Mind affects your Body. Your state of mind has been shown to affect your blood pressure, sweat glands, production of adrenaline and many other body functions which, taken together, have a very significant effect on your health and resistance to illness.

Body affects Mind. The condition of your body has a strong influence on your mind, as exhausted students taking a test or any drunk driver can readily confirm.

In 1975 *The Relaxation Response* by Herbert Benson showed the results of a remarkable study at Harvard Medical School. It demonstrated clearly, and with medically-accepted accuracy, the body's response to reducing mental tension. Conditions harmful to the body, including high blood pressure, were shown to decrease significantly simply by the process of relaxing.

Body - Relationships

Your Body affects your Relationships. A beautiful body does amazing things in terms of attracting people and sustaining relationships. The ability, or inability, to participate in social activities, sports and sex have a similar effect.

Relationships affect Body. Improving social or sexual relationships is a major motivation for many people to spend time in the gym or follow diets, and the result is often a visible difference in their body.

Dean Ornish, the doctor whose widely acclaimed program helps people with deteriorating heart conditions regain active lives, addresses the body-relationship connection in his new book *Love & Survival*. Surprisingly, there is already research evidence showing the healing effect of intimacy and relationships.

Relationships - Career

Your Relationships affect your Career. This connection is exemplified in the popular saying, "It's not what you know, it's who you know." Relationships are an essential part of advancing your career.

Career affects Relationships. Work is a great place to meet people, and many of a person's relationships develop there. This may include *the* relationship, which leads to marriage. The same is true of unpaid careers such as being an avid skier or student.

Since your unpaid careers include your long-term, avid interests (*skiing, social club, art*) it's only natural that the people you meet while doing them are the ones most likely to share your deep interests. You're quite likely to be compatible, look forward to seeing each other, and always have something interesting to talk about.

Body - Career

Your Body affects your Career. This is important not only for athletes who need a strong body to pursue their career. If you're too sick to go to work, or don't have the stamina to work the necessary hours, your career can be severely affected.

Career affects Body. If your career involves physical activity, it can shape up your body without any extra effort on your part. If your job involves sitting all day, you can end up overweight, low on energy and a candidate for an early heart attack.

The people who rise to the top of almost every profession or field of endeavor are usually in good shape. This doesn't mean athletic, but it does mean fit and healthy. They make good impressions and tend to be alert, active and energetic as they advance new ideas, projects and programs. Without that energy they wouldn't be able to lead the people, issues and organizations which make them stand out.

Surroundings - Body

Your Surroundings affect your Body. If you're surrounded by a cold, drafty, unclean environment you're more likely to have colds and other health problems. If you live in a mountainous area, you may have to do some vigorous walking and be in better physical shape.

Body affects Surroundings. People with physical problems are sometimes limited in where they can live. People who are strong and energetic are able to easily maintain and improve their surroundings.

Imagine a boy huddled in a one-room apartment without heat, shivering while flies buzz around garbage in the corner and several family members share the room with him, coughing and wiping runny noses. Now imagine a girl playing in a comfortable living room where she can see a clean kitchen and hear family members down the hall in their rooms, none of them coughing or sneezing. Which surroundings are more likely to produce the healthy child?

Surroundings - Mind

Your Surroundings affect your Mind. It's well known that getting away from the hurly-burly of daily life to a quiet, beautiful place can help you relax and regain your peace of mind.

Mind affects Surroundings. When you achieve some peace of mind you gain a better understanding of how to make your surroundings comfortable, have fewer arguments and defuse tensions around you.

Imagine finishing a long, difficult day at work and driving home through aggravating rush-hour traffic. In the driveway you slam the car door and ignore a neighbor waving at you from across the street. In the house you change clothes and head out the back door into a forested park. Sunlight filters through the trees. You start to relax. A squirrel runs beside you and you can't help laughing at his antics. You see a woman you know. You smile and wave; she waves back.... One of your neighbors saw a grouch, the other saw a happy person. Did your surroundings make a difference?

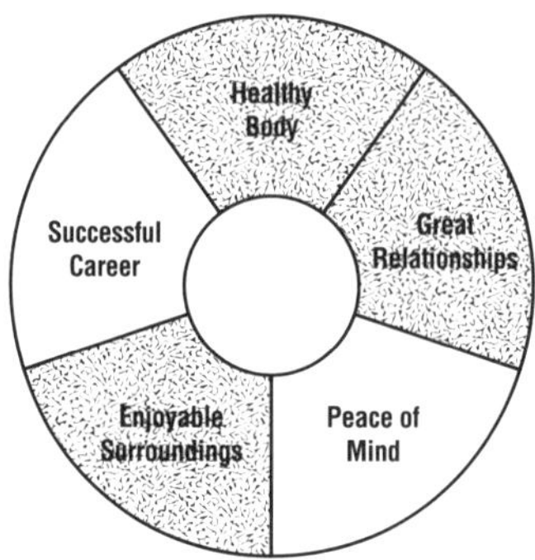

Mind - Career

Your Mind affects your Career. Being level-headed, happy and sometimes excited about what you do for a living goes a long way toward making you successful.

Career affects Mind. If you've chosen a career that you like doing — and you should — you find you're not just earning money, you're bringing something good into the world. You gain satisfaction and well-earned pride.

I know a graphics artist who does amazing work. He has every conceivable type font, and if those aren't good enough, he makes his own. Scanners, processors and printers compete with piles of references for space in his loft. With most graphics people, you hope their work will be up to what you want. With Jim it's always better than you expected. Why? He loves his work. He talks about it, reads about it, collects other people's work and experiments with his own. When he finishes a job it's not just something to send out the door; he keeps a copy to enjoy. And why not? It's excellent.

Career - Surroundings

Your Career affects your Surroundings. Earning money lets you buy good things to keep around yourself. Business travel and unpaid careers—like being an avid hiker—can produce photos and other collectibles that add style to your life.

Surroundings affect Career. Personal impressions make a big difference in your career. These are strongly influenced by your personal effects such as clothing, car, office décor and home. In addition, you'll find your opportunities are different in New York City than in Boise, Idaho.

I told you about Jim's graphics materials covering every inch around him. Were these surroundings good for his career? I guess so, judging by the results.

A friend who is a businessman could not be more different. His home is sparsely decorated with sculpted stone and formed metal, all made by his own hand. And they're of gallery quality. People who visit him on business come away amazed at his multiple talents, and their admiration for him rises accordingly.

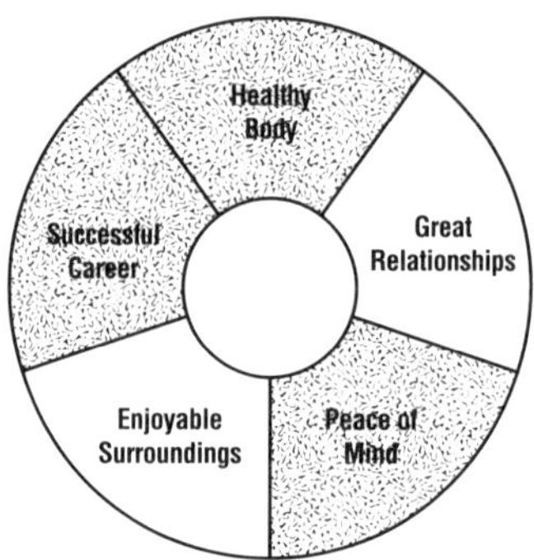

Relationships - Surroundings

Your Relationships affect your Surroundings. Marriage leads to sharing your home and possessions with someone else, which has a definite effect on your surroundings. Even having roommates who share the rent can make a big difference.

Surroundings affect Relationships. Most people clearly recognize this link. That's why they choose different surroundings—clothes, restaurants, etc.—depending on who they're with and what their relationship is.

Surroundings send clear messages about relationships. Consider:

You visit a friend you once dated. The lights are low, candles are lit, soft music is playing. Do you sense a desire to re-kindle the relationship?

Or, you come home to the apartment you've been sharing with your live-in partner. All your belongings are in the hall and the lock has been changed. Is this relationship changing?

Relationships - Mind

Your Relationships affect your Mind. Having friends who stand by you makes a tremendous difference. Especially when you're upset, angry or just need a shoulder to cry on. It helps you regain your peace of mind and face the world again.

Mind affects Relationships. If you're able to not lash out in anger, and instead be the soothing person others turn to in their time of need, and are the person to have fun with, you'll attract and keep many friends.

Years ago I had just left one job and was starting another; it was a very unsettling time. A friend came over for the afternoon and we sat in the backyard and talked. I remember she seemed so OK with the world. We laughed about one thing and another. After she left, everything was all right. The answers I needed began to appear one after another. I also recall times she needed someone to be there, and how she appreciated those times together. Life is great. That's what friends are for.

Bernie Siegel's Gardener

Bernie Siegel is a caring medical doctor who specializes in treating cancer patients. In the course of performing this emotionally draining work, he discovered something truly exceptional. Many of the people who survived the onset of cancer had a completely different approach to life than those who died. He documented these intriguing insights of a mind-body connection in his bestseller *Peace, Love and Healing*. In it, he tells the story of a gardener who came to him with a diagnosis of cancer and, as the referring doctor put it, an immediate need for surgery.

Yet the gardener told Dr. Siegel the surgery would have to be delayed. Why? Because it was springtime. The man loved his gardening, and loved making the world beautiful in that way. He figured if he survived, that would be great. But if not, he'd leave behind a beautiful world.

Dr. Siegel was perplexed but, after giving his usual medical advice, had to go along with the man's wishes.

Weeks later the gardener showed up, happy to have so much of his work done, and ready for treatment. The surgery went well. He remained in good spirits and healed quickly. But a medical report found considerable cancer remained throughout his body.

He declined chemotherapy, wanting to get back to his gardening and his life.

Four years later, the gardener called on Bernie Siegel again. The doctor was shocked. Without the additional treatment, there was almost no way the man could have survived. Yet there he was.

And the visit had nothing to do with cancer. The eighty-two-year-old gardener had a hernia from lifting boulders. The man refused to be admitted to a hospital, so the work was done under local anesthesia. With that, the gardener went back to his work and his life.

Dr. Siegel used this as a clear example of the mind-body connection, and it is.

But it's also much more.

Using what you know about the LifeCycle, do you see anything else?

What about the man's career and his body? Was he laying at home in bed? Or was he being active at work and giving his body a chance to function normally?

Did his surroundings of beautiful flowers contribute to his peace of mind?

How about the relationship he had with Dr. Siegel? Did he seem like a victim? Did he seem like an oppressor? Can you imagine him having many friends who appreciate his love of life and nature—people who stand by him in time of need?

The gardener took advantage of all the sources of strength in his life. He used all the connections, and let each part of his life support the others in an incredibly resilient network.

When we were young, most of us were taught to solve problems by doing the obvious thing: take action within one part of our life. When we have a health problem, we treat it with a health cure.

Dr. Siegel and others have gone farther, opening up the benefits of the mind-body connection to help people overcome problems with their health. The additional energy and healing it creates is a valuable gift to the people who receive it.

Now you can go even farther. You can open up the benefits of the many LifeCycle connections in your life. The small miracle Dr. Siegel's gardener experienced should not be the exception. These small miracles should start happening much more often. And not be limited to health, but include relationships, peace of mind, career and surroundings.

The way to do it is shown here. And it's yours if you want it.

Key Word

The easiest way I've found to get started is to look at the exercise you did on page 19 and re-read the things you'd like to bring into your life. Do that now, to refresh those good ideas.

With those things in mind, pick a word you'd like to have associated with yourself. A word that would make you feel good if people think of it when they see you.

Here are some of the words people have chosen and used. Pick one of these or come up with your own.

Caring	Witty	Successful	Artist
Excellent	Intelligent	Creative	Educator
Sexy	Leader	Professional	Cheerful
Wealthy	Down home	Famous	Spiritual
Healthy	Popular	Religious	Expert
Athletic	Mom	Confident	Knowledgeable
Author	Dad	Youthful	World traveler
Influential	Wife	Attractive	
Social leader	Husband	Fun	

There may be several words you'd enjoy having applied to yourself. For now, just pick one—the one that would really make you feel good if you were considered exceptional in this way.

Write your word here:______________________________

This word is your key. We're going to use it to unlock some great things in your life, one step at a time.

Small Steps

The major reason for failure in any endeavor in life is that the things we want seem as if they're at the top of stone towers like the ones which protect castles. You can see what you want up there, and other people are up there enjoying that life already, but there's no apparent way to climb or jump high enough to get there.

So most people give up: the failed diet, the lost career opportunity, the relationship that didn't work, the house they couldn't afford, the emotional roller-coaster they couldn't get off.

The secret is to look for the small step. A thing you **can** do. And do it. The result is much like going inside that tall tower and taking the stairs. One small step at a time, higher and higher, until you reach the top.

Remember the word you selected? It's something worth having, something that can make you stand out among other people. It's like that tall tower—by taking the first few steps of the LifeCycle process you'll start to move up quickly. From there, you can look out through windows and see you're a little higher than when you started. If you want to go higher, you can. If you want it enough, you can go all the way to the top.

Your steps begin with the next chapter.

Healthy Body

Now that you have a good starting place, you're ready to go to the next level. We're going to develop a deeper understanding of the five parts of your life. Then you'll see how to start using each of them to get what you want in life.

There are a few basic keys to building up a **healthy body** and a healthy life. To understand them we need to look at the things that wear your body down. Then we can look at how to develop the body, health and life you want.

I'm sure you already know quite a bit about your health and your body. Recognizing that, I'm going to briefly cover some "things everyone knows," then add some things that are not as well known. After that, we'll bring it all together into a clearer view of your overall health and life.

Almost everyone takes their body for granted. You're born with it. It's always there, every day. You feed it junk food and it survives. You get sick and your body recovers nicely. You get little or no sleep for long periods of time and your body muddles through.

But it takes a toll. When you were a child and a teenager, your body grew and repaired itself at such a prodigious rate that almost anything you did to your body—if it didn't kill you—was OK. Your body would spring right back to normal.

Up to your mid-twenties your body has a freshness which contributes to your attractiveness, energy and athletic ability. After that, your body continues to heal itself, but at a slower rate. Unfortunately, the bad habits we learn when we're young and indestructible stay with us. Lack of sleep, fatty foods, minimal exercise, continuous reliance on drugs of the legal or illegal variety—all make it difficult for your body to do its work and repair the damage.

Inevitably, then, your body begins to run out of energy sooner, your skin develops wrinkles and begins to sag, your hair begins to thin, your joints become less flexible, and your vision isn't what it used to be. The worst part is...this all starts happening in your thirties.

Your body continues to become less appealing and deteriorates until it sputters to a stop in your seventies.

That's what happens to the average person.

It doesn't have to happen to you.

Researchers into longevity such as Roy Walford at UCLA believe that the human body as it currently exists is capable of sustaining life until 120 years of age or longer. Gene researchers are working to push this figure even higher, but that's in the future. How would you like to begin extending your seventy-some years—starting today?

Better yet, how would you like to extend more of your peak-form health from your twenties into all the years of your life: the energy, flexibility, quick recovery, attractiveness, sexuality and athletic ability.

You can do it.

Don't get me wrong. Your body does wear down...but the rate can be **much** slower than what most people routinely accept today.

In fact, for people who try the LifeCycle process and stay with it for several months, it's not unusual to get compliments that they're looking younger or more attractive. They're not younger, of course, but may well be more attractive. As your body improves inside, it's reflected in your skin, muscle tone and energy—which people automatically associate with youth, sex and vitality. If that's what other people think, that's not a problem.

To understand why those things happen, let's take a closer look at how your body works.

First, your body takes in nutrients in the form of food and air. It extracts raw material from them: oxygen, minerals, vitamins and other molecules needed to support all of your body's functions. Those basic functions include replacing old cells with new ones (*growth, healing*), producing necessary fluids (*blood, lymph*), producing energy (*muscle movement, etc.*) and expelling waste.

But the really interesting part is the complex, second-level functions. This includes activities performed by your brain and central nervous system (*conscious thought, subconscious body control, pain-detection*), your eyes (*sight*), internal organs (*reproduction, digestion, breathing, blood-filtering*) and glands (*hormone production and other secretions that adjust the body's functions*).

To appreciate what this means, consider that we can't duplicate all those things in a laboratory. We can put a person on the Moon, and build an Internet that covers the world. But we're unable to build a robot that performs all the functions your body can do.

Yet a man, a woman and a bottle of wine are all it takes to create another person tonight. And, actually, you can get by without the wine.

That gives you some idea of the enormous power you have at your fingertips. And not just reproduction. How about preventing illnesses?

Most of the time, your body fights off an illness and you're not even aware of it. No matter where you live, there are germs, spores and bacteria in the air around you, every day. They're in the ground, on your pets and around your home. But you don't get sick every day. Why?

Because your body's incredible immune system meets germs and infections at the point of contact and goes to work on them—in your stomach, in your lungs and on your skin. You never even notice it. Your body does this naturally every day.

If infection gets into your bloodstream or elsewhere in your body, you often notice it. Your temperature may rise, inflammation can occur and other symptoms may develop. Much of the time, you could ignore it and continue with your life. You just experience some pain and reduced effectiveness for a few days, then it all goes away. It's happened to me. It's probably happened to you, when no medicine was at hand. Your body cures itself.

Sometimes illness may hit so hard you're leveled and have to stay in bed. Even so, your body fights off the illness and eventually puts you back on your feet. But—sometimes not. Some illnesses can kill you. Which is why knowing about medicine is a good idea.

Why not take medicine all the time, whenever something comes up?

There are a few simple reasons, which any medical doctor can confirm:

○ If you take some medicines too often, they lose their effectiveness *(penicillin, etc.)*

○ If you take drugs repeatedly, your body can become addicted to them *(painkillers, etc.)*

○ If you use medicines every time a condition comes up, your body can become dependent on it, and stop producing its own normal responses

○ Under some conditions, side effects and complications from medicine can be more injurious than the original problem, and may even be lethal. That's why prescription medicines are controlled substances

Does this mean you should never take medicine? Some people make that choice. More people simply come to the realization that you should use medicine judiciously...and far less often than most people use it today.

If you want to live a healthier, longer life, look for ways to strengthen your body's already incredible immune system. Use the mildest possible medication that will get you through the illness. The same way exercise strengthens your muscles, this simple course of treatment strengthens your body's immune defenses. And makes it harder for illness to get a foothold the next time.

How well do "alternative" courses of treatment work? The growing acceptance and use of herbal remedies and alternative treatments is one of the clearest indications that people are getting successful results. American Medical Association journals like the Archives of Internal Medicine have published studies showing such treatments can be effective, including use of ginger to prevent nausea in pregnant women, ginko biloba to improve cognitive functions of Alzheimer's patients, and saw palmetto to treat enlarged prostates.

The main attraction for herbal remedies and alternative treatment is that they are more "natural" than prescription medications. As a result they tend to have less of a sudden impact on the body. Treatments that are gentle and yet effective make a lot of sense.

But the best cure is still "prevention."

Getting your body in more of a healthy state can dramatically reduce the number of times you get sick.

When you do get ill, becoming more adept with gentle treatments and starting them right away can head-off the need for antibiotics and other strong medicines.

Having check-ups as often as your health plan or wallet will allow is also a good idea, to catch any major health problem and start treatment as soon as possible before it gets out of hand.

Exercise is a great idea if you can make it enjoyable (*walking, tennis, volleyball, etc.*) or at least something you don't mind doing. Any activity is great. Then moving it up a notch is even better.

The same is true for food. People often try extreme diets for a short time then drop them. Instead, just start eating better, one step at a time.

What we're talking about here is how to move from health problems to health strengths. In other words, taking those parts of your health that are holding you back physically, mentally and every other way, and unlocking the energy and vitality that will let you excel.

Steps

Now let's look at some things you can do with all this—ways to bring the benefits of good health into your life.

Remember the word you chose in the previous chapter? Think of some small **things** you could acquire which would remind people of that word. For now, just consider things related to having a healthy body. Jot them here.

Examples: related books on that subject, photos, souvenirs, certificates, sports equipment, clothes, posters, tools-of-the-trade, magazines, music, household items, office items, and cards-letters-gifts from others.

Things

you

could

acquire

Now think of some things or activities in your life the way it is today, which suggest the **opposite** of that word. Remember we're just looking at your health and body at this point. Jot those here.

Opposite

of

your

word

Next, think of some **skills** you could acquire, or ongoing **activities** you could do—related to having a healthy body—which would remind people of the word you chose. Note those here.

<table>
<tr><td>Skills</td><td></td></tr>
<tr><td>and</td><td></td></tr>
<tr><td>activities</td><td></td></tr>
</table>

For example, if you picked the word **wealthy** you might have come up with thoughts on the three lists which include items like the ones below. Note that these are very small steps that almost anyone could do.

Health   You've been exercising in your garage. You could get a membership at an upscale gym. (*Not an expensive, exclusive club unless you can afford it. Stay within your means.*)

You don't know which end of a golf club to hold. You could buy a reasonable set of clubs, get five relatively inexpensive lessons and be a week-end golf player.

If for some reason you find you're not really interested in doing the things you identified, pick another word that works better for you. The things you come up with should be relatively easy and things you could see yourself doing.

Now go over your three lists above:

Acquire: things you might get

Opposite: things you might fix

Activities: things you might do

Add any new thoughts which occur to you.

Next, pick **one** thing from the lists which meets these criteria: it's something you could do easily and soon, without too much cost.

Copy that one item here

Health: _______________________________

Great! Save this step and we'll come back to it.

You're well on your way. Let's enjoy exploring some other parts of your life before we get down to the equally enjoyable work of making things better in your life. You'll find this exploring also opens up some positive things in your life. Onward!

Great Relationships

One of the most important things in your life is relationships. Family and friends, lovers and losers, the highest and lowest points in our lives have a lot to do with the people close to us. And sometimes, the strangest things happen in relationships. Let's take a look behind the scenes to see what's going on.

Over the years, I've had the good fortune to travel in many countries around the world and develop relationships with people in many cultures. The most striking thing about those relationships is not how much they're different, but how much they're the same.

Born in New York, I've lived in California, Arizona, Maryland, Vermont and Massachusetts—plus Japan and Germany. Various jobs and a sense of adventure have taken me to Mexico, Canada, England, France, Belgium,

Switzerland, Italy, Israel, Jordan, Egypt, Denmark, Sweden and The Netherlands.

In all these countries, even when I could only speak a few words of the local language, I was still able to have great relationships with people I met. From these experiences I came to realize the two basic attributes people have which affect all their relationships:

Each of us has aspects of our lives and personalities which are **in front** and seen by other people. We also have aspects which are **in back** and not seen as often.

The things we put in front are many and varied. And they're strongly affected by the people around us. This is where most of the differences exist between people in different lands, cultures, ethnic groups, age groups and economic groups.

The things in back are amazingly similar among all of us, no matter where we are in the world. We all grow up in families and usually have relationships with parents, brothers/sisters and other relatives. We develop relationships with people of the same sex. We develop relationships with people of the opposite sex. Sex happens. Either we or our friends have children. We form career relationships and social relationships. And we deal with changes—good and bad—to those relationships.

Those things are true whether your home is Paris, France or Paris, Texas...York, England or New York City...Little Tokyo in Los Angeles or Tokyo, Japan.

In Front

What are the things we put in front, and how do they affect our relationships?

Each of us starts with a set of physical characteristics (*height, sex, weight, eye color, hair color, etc.*) but even those can be changed. While sex change is not common, it's not impossible. If people feel they are too tall or too short, they wear lower heels or higher heels, stand up straighter or slouch down. People diet to slim down and take additives to bulk up. Eye color is changed with contact lenses. Hair color comes in a bottle.

This is not to say any of these things are good or bad. They're just things people do.

The list of things we put in front goes on. Staying with physical aspects for a moment, it includes all the clothes we put on—choosing color, fit and style to project a different image at different times: casual, dressed-up, athletic, sexy, professional, wedding-day fancy. And accessories make a statement: tattoos, diamonds, baseball cap, piercings, sunglasses, Rolex watch. All reflect a desire by the person wearing them to belong to a certain group, to be accepted at a certain level. And it's amazing how often it works.

We also put in front who we "are"—songwriter, doctor, mother, social leader, computer expert or actor. Add to that our special interests—avid skier, rock musician, ethnic food chef, world traveler, painter or antique collector.

It's a simple fact of life that some of these things are true and reflect who we are. Others are not true and reflect who we would like to be. This common habit of stretching the truth is not necessarily a bad thing. It depends on what we do about it.

Each of us grows by wanting to be better at something in the future than we are today. In high school, if you wanted to be an airline pilot, teacher, musician or business owner, you were told that's a good thing. It's called ambition, wanting to grow and accomplish something. The same is true today.

If you make up songs and sing them to your dog—then tell people you're a songwriter—that's a stretch. If you write the songs down, it's a step in the right direction. By some definitions, that makes you a songwriter. By professional standards, you'd have to sell or publish a song before you're a professional songwriter. Maybe that's your next goal. But as long as you're working on it and making progress, you justify that slight exaggeration. You're being a songwriter.

As the LifeCycle process will show you, success in becoming the person you want to be has little to do with luck. Luck mostly determines when and how you succeed. Whether you succeed has more to do with whether you're working on it—and how you're going about it.

If you put something "in front" and don't take steps to make it real, there's good news and bad news. The good news is: you'll actually have some small successes. The bad news is: eventually you crash and burn.

Simple pretense is great at parties. It may even work for the first few stages of a relationship. But if you're pretending to be a movie director, eventually people expect to see your films. If you don't have any, you have to pack your bags and start over somewhere else. A significant number of people make their living this way, failing and moving on.

The alternative is very simple. Whatever you put "in front," take steps to do it and make it real. If you do, it moves from pretense to reality.

Successful Relationships #1

The actual steps you take to improve relationships along with all the other parts of your life are coming soon. For now, here are some things "everyone knows" but aren't often practiced—yet they're surprisingly effective.

The essential cornerstone, of course, is to pay attention to the other person. But with a twist: What are they putting "in front?" Be interested. Ask and listen. Then remember. It makes a tremendous difference to people if you remember these things about them.

Accept what you learn about them. Try not to judge what they put in front—whether that's their real hair color or they actually have a Ph.D. Who cares? In the long run it works itself out.

In fact, do the opposite. Acknowledge what they put in front. Maybe even compliment it. I know, this seems fairly obvious. But you'd be amazed how much people appreciate it. And how rarely it's given to them.

These small, introductory things are important—especially with initial relationships, short relationships, social relationships, work relationships and initial sexual relationships.

In Back

What are the things we keep "in back" which affect our relationships? As I mentioned earlier, the most basic of these are the family things we grow up with—relationships with parents and family members. Added to this are the big and little experiences children have—the gift-giving events, playing with friends, successes, failures, embarrassments, bullies. Everyone has experienced these things. Even though we present to the world a grown-up appearance, these things are still there.

And those experiences don't stop with our younger years. Through our teens and twenties—when each of us take charge of our own life—wrenching changes are caused by things like moving away from home, sexual relationships and jobs. These successes and failures, fears and put-downs, freedom and finally having money are also shared by most people in one form or another.

For some it continues to a new family life with spouse and children. Significant changes happen in a person's life after marriage, including pregnancy and dealing with the demands and joys of having children. For those who go this way, the raw experiences and feelings are remarkably similar wherever you travel across the country or around the world.

Other things that people have "in back" are: concerns for their health, their weight, their appearance. Desires to get ahead in their social standing, in their work, in the quality of things they have. Questions about life, whether there's an afterlife, issues about religion. Wondering which direction to go in their life, how long they'll live, what will bring success and happiness.

Everyone wrestles with issues like these at some time or another.

Even though these things don't often sit on the surface of people's thoughts, they can be tremendously important and can seriously affect their relationships.

Sometimes, your ability to have a relationship with another person may have very little to do with you. That sounds strange, but let me give you some examples.

For no apparent reason, one of your neighbors doesn't like you. You may be completely unaware they had an on-going fight with the person who previously lived there, and have never gotten over it.

Another example: a man drinking at a bar finds he can't please a woman he meets there. He doesn't know her father often came home drunk and hit her. If he meets her while standing in line at a movie theater, it can have a completely different outcome. Being unaware of what a person has "in back" can have a major effect on your relationship with them.

There is also a strong tendency for people to develop "us" versus "them" relationships. This is a tribal thing historians have traced back thousands of years. People banded together to protect themselves against wild animals and dangerous people who might kill them or steal from them. Even today, we subconsciously sort people into "us" and "them."

People we see as "us" are trusted and we share things with them. Close relationships can develop. People we see as "them" are suspect and kept at a distance. Close relationships with "them" are almost impossible.

Fortunately, there are things that can be done to handle what people have "in back."

Successful Relationships #2

To develop a deeper, stronger relationship with someone, you have to go beyond the things "in front" and deal with what they have "in back." This takes real effort, but the rewards are fantastic.

It starts with simple conversation. What's their background? If they don't volunteer it, ask them in a friendly manner. Listen. Then share some of your background and experiences.

When you do this, you'll almost always find something the two of you have in common. This makes the relationship more fun and rewarding for you—and does the same for them.

Gradually, the two of you can become "we." And the more "in back" bonds you develop, the stronger the relationship becomes.

There are good ways to develop these bonds. The LifeCycle process gives you a good start down this path. Let's look at that now.

Steps

Similar to what we did in the previous section, let's consider some things you can do to bring the benefit of great relationships into your life.

Think of some small **things** you could acquire which would remind people of the word you identified earlier.

For now, just focus on things related to having good relationships. Jot them here.

> *Examples: related books on that subject, photos, souvenirs, certificates, sports equip-ment, clothes, posters, tools-of-the-trade, magazines, music, household items, office items, and cards-letters-gifts from others.*

Things _______________________________

you _______________________________

could _______________________________

acquire _______________________________

Now think of some things or activities in your life the way it is today, which suggest the **opposite** of that word. Remember we're only addressing your relationships at this point. Jot those here.

Opposite _______________________________

of _______________________________

your _______________________________

word _______________________________

Next, think of some **skills** you could acquire, or ongoing **activities** you could do—related to having good relationships—which would remind people of the word you chose. Note those here.

Skills

and

activities

To give an example in this area, if you picked the word **wealthy** you might have come up with thoughts on the three lists like these.

Relationships

Jot down the names of some people you know who have wealthy relatives or friends. Invite one of your friends and their well-to-do relative to dinner at a nice restaurant. Enjoy that world for an evening. You may even get an invitation in return.

When you can afford it, do it again with different people.

Now go over your three lists above:

Acquire: things you might get

Opposite: things you might fix

Activities: things you might do

Add any new thoughts which occur to you.

As before, pick **one** thing from the lists which meets these criteria: it's something you could do easily and soon, without too much cost.

Copy that one item here.

Relationships:

____

Excellent! Save this step and we'll come back to it.

That's real progress. You'll find developing these ideas and steps will become easier each time. On to the next!

Successful Career

As I mentioned earlier, your career is what you do. For most people this involves working for someone else and getting a regular paycheck. But it also includes being self-employed, a student, homemaker, social leader or contract worker (*such as an actor*). With few modifications, the same elements apply to improving whatever career you have or want to have.

Just about everyone has several careers. Sometimes simultaneously, sometimes one after another. You may be paid for them, you may not. Either way, they're careers.

Being a mother is a career. You work hard, produce children and raise them, and support all the members of the family.

Being a student is a career. With any luck at all, it will be followed by another career. But for many years, that's what you do in life.

Or you may be a hospital administrator who's worked at three different hospitals in the last six years. That's your career. At the same time, you may be very much into painting. You've been painting for twelve years, finally got some of your work into a gallery last year and actually sold two. That's a career also. In fact, you may find that you put more time and avid interest into your painting than into your day job. Then if a television talk-show host likes your paintings, this could become your full-time career.

Recognizing your career and doing something about it can produce tremendous results and satisfaction in your life.

The Right Career

There are two kinds of careers: those you do because you have to, and those you do because you want to.

You're more likely to be successful if you do the one you want to do. You're also likely to be happier doing it.

Easier said than done? At first, probably true. When each of us gets started in life we often "fall into" the work we do. You need money, the job's available, and you can do it. Years later you look around and you're still doing it.

For some people the thing they fall into is what their parents or relatives do for a living.

Or it may be something you liked in school so you took classes in it and looked for a job in that field. This is a step in the right direction, but usually doesn't get you where you really want to go.

Why is getting started in the right career so difficult?

One major reason is we don't really know what the choices are. We've heard **some** career titles—certainly not all of them. We may even see someone doing a career we're interested in. But that's not the same as knowing what it's like to do that career every day for the next thirty years.

In fact, at first we don't know what it's like to do any paid career. Until we've held a steady job, we can't guess what it's like. Until you've been doing it several years and gotten (*or not gotten*) raises and a promotion, how do you know how the system works? Until you've seen how career tracks actually run in the real world, how do you know you're doing it the right way or wrong way?

The logical place to learn all these things is in school. That's where we get prepared to start careers, right? But for whatever reason, our schools tend to teach subjects rather than careers.

English, math and history are not careers. Nor are chemistry, business, law or engineering.

Some actual careers in law, for example, are law clerk, lawyer, judge and legislator. Of them, only the clerk's job has a close resemblance to what students do in law school. Several friends who are lawyers (*I admit it, some of my friends are*) assure me the real skills they use every day are the ability to get people to do what the lawyer wants them to do (*clients, juries, witnesses*), the ability to be confrontational in the right way, acting ability, and the ability to bring in new business (*in private practice*) or be an assembly-line worker (*in public practice*). As it turns out, large numbers of people go into law and then give it up when they discover what it's really like.

In fact, I've found most people are not currently working in the field they studied in school. Of those who are in that field, a majority of them feel stuck in a position that's not really what they want to do.

Yet many people each year successfully make a transition into what they really want to do. This may be a step you want to take at some point.

If so, the way to get there is fairly straightforward. First, consider what you'd **really** like to do to earn a living. Do you already know what it is? If so, great. If not, it may be time to start thinking about it.

What are your unpaid careers and strong interests? What do you enjoy talking about? Is there something you always wanted to do but put off? If there's a paying career in any of these areas, give it some serious consideration.

Recognize that some people have careers they really enjoy. They made the transition and they're doing it. Imagine yourself completing that transition. Imagine yourself doing the career you want, and loving it.

Next, get some accurate information on career transition. A very good book on this subject is ***What Color Is Your Parachute?*** by Richard Nelson Bolles; it's easy to read and has some great material.

Then, use the LifeCycle process to begin doing something about it.

As I mentioned earlier, be sure to use small steps in your journey. For example, if you want to be a Hollywood actor, don't quit your office job in Dubuque, Iowa and move to Hollywood to live on unemployment while waiting for a big break. Living in Los Angeles for many years, I've known people who tried it that way. As any director will tell you, it's much better to keep the day job for now and get on a local cable show in Dubuque. Almost anyone can. It gives you a little exposure, some credits and video footage to go with your résumé. Then break into a local TV program or an independent film produced in the Mid-West, even if it goes direct-to-video—it's more exposure, more credits and more video footage.

That's the right time to get an agent and try to land some auditions for big-time TV or movie roles. If and when it makes sense to go live in Hollywood and do serious auditions, don't forget your day-job skills. It helps to have money to spend so you can schmooze with people in the movie business for as long as it takes. As it happens, I knew Jenna Elfman prior to her big break with *Dharma and Greg.* She worked at it for a long time before she became an "overnight success."

Moving Up

If you're already doing what you really like to do or plan to stick with your current job for a while, make the best of it. There are ways to move up and be more successful, which you might want to consider. As long as you're putting effort into what you do, why not be good at it and be well rewarded?

Most people take the same approach in their career that they used in school: show up each day, do what they're told, and hope to move ahead.

That still works for clerical jobs and positions in government. It also worked years ago when you stayed in one company for your whole career. But it really doesn't work for most careers any more.

Today, following the "school" approach often gets you stuck in a dead-end position with less compensation, recognition and satisfaction than you really want in what you do for a living.

A successful career today is based primarily on three things: having some area of expertise relevant to your work, developing relationships, and being ready to move to your next job *inside or outside your present organization*.

In the past, your expertise was the basic qualification for a career. It was based primarily on "been doing it so many years I know it forward and backward." Now, the college degree (*if any*) and previous experience are not enough. Things change so quickly—especially with computer and communication innovations springing up everywhere—that success leans heavier on "what have you done for me lately?"

This new emphasis requires on-the-job training and off-site courses to keep you valuable. On-the-job development is something you do yourself—mostly asking questions about things you don't know, getting into details, and doing it yourself one or more times. That keeps your expertise up with the people around you.

Off-site courses are offered by colleges and private training schools on every subject from personal computers to sales to acting. They can be as short as a three-hour class or as extensive as a graduate degree; most are just a few days or evenings. These can give you a level of expertise beyond the people you work with—which adds to your personal satisfaction and value. They are also great for justifying raises and promotions. And they look very good on your resume when you want to change jobs.

Relationships are taking on growing importance. At critical points in your career they surpass expertise in terms of realizing your goals and dreams. I'm sure it comes as no surprise that relationships with your boss—and their boss—are important. But it's also important to have good relationships with other high level people in the organization, with people at the same level as yourself, with the people who work for you and, more than ever before, with people outside your company.

Equally important with expertise and relationships is transition. As we discussed, working at one job for your whole career is something you see in museums alongside dinosaurs. For better or for worse, almost all jobs are short-term now. Every few years you're likely to move up, move sideways or move out of the organization. Being ready to transition to your next job is essential.

To get that next job, someone has to hire you or include you in their organization. This is where relationships with people other than your boss become important. To get ready for this, consider who you know—or would like to know—who has the ability to hire you. Meet those people...or re-new those acquaintances if you knew them before. Improve those relationships and raise them to another level.

Your current job will end some day. Be ready and have avenues open so that when the inevitable happens, your life will go on. In fact, if your present position isn't your ideal situation, don't wait for it to happen. Your relationships will eventually turn up a better offer. That offer may be all it takes to get your present boss to see the light and transform your job so it's much more to your liking. If not, ring out the old and ring in the new.

Your career should be an upward journey, bringing you more of what's important to you. It means a lot to your whole life and happiness. It's worth doing right.

Power of the Right Career

If you have a flickering interest in doing a career you really like, let me throw a little more wood on the fire.

There are very clear reasons why people are more successful doing what they enjoy. You know you're doing a career you really like when:

○ You know more about your field than other people because you're truly interested in it. You're always soaking up more information during your spare time—because it's not work, it's fun. You read articles about it, buy things related to it, and do recreational things that are related in some way.

○ You develop friends in the field—people who enjoy talking about your shared interest. These people often turn out to be great resources later when you're faced with a new problem or opportunity in your line of work.

○ You tend to be more imaginative and creative in this field than other people—because of the wide variety of information and insights you've gained over the years from experience, reading and personal conversations.

○ You have more energy than other people in the field because you love being there. This is what you enjoy doing. You rarely get tired doing it. You're still going, creating and accomplishing things when others have run down. Which of you is going to be more successful?

○ Last, and certainly not least, you're happier doing it, and living a more complete life. Your career isn't competing with your personal relationships, your health, where you want to be, or your peace of mind. In fact, your career supports all the other parts of your life, and they in turn raise your career even higher.

Steps

With all that in mind, let's identify some things you can do with all this—ways to bring the benefits of a successful career into your life.

Think of some small **things** you could acquire which would remind people of the word you chose earlier. For now, just focus on things related to your career(s). Jot them here.

Things

you

could

acquire

Now think of some things or activities in your life the way it is today, which suggest the **opposite** of that word. Remember we're only looking at your career at this point. Jot those here.

Opposite

of

your

word

Next, think of some **skills** you could acquire, or ongoing **activities** you could do—related to having a successful career—which would remind people of the word you chose. Note those here.

Skills

and

activities

For example, if you picked the word **wealthy** you might have come up with thoughts on the three lists like these.

Career   Your workplace or office is full of junk. You could clean it and put in some golf things or similar items.

Your clothes are OK but not quite up to others at the office. You could buy one very good outfit and wear it on special occasions.

Now go over your three lists above:

Acquire: things you might get

Opposite: things you might fix

Activities: things you might do

Add any new thoughts which occur to you.

Like you did before, pick **one** thing from the lists which meets these criteria: it's something you could do easily and soon, without too much cost.

Copy that one item here.

Career:

Very good! Save this step and we'll come back to it.

In the course of developing these steps you may be surprised by some of the things you come up with. That's good. It shows you're broadening your horizons and expanding your growth opportunities.

Enjoyable Surroundings

Your surroundings have a lot to do with your ability to enjoy your life. They also are a major influence on the people around you—as well as on their opinion about you. It's definitely an important part of your life.

Surroundings include everything outside your body. It starts with your clothes and any jewelry, sunglasses, etc. It includes your car, motorcycle or other vehicle. It includes your home and everything in it, whether or not it belongs to you. It's everything at the place you work, whether it's yours or not. It's everything outdoors that you ever see—to or from work, on your own time, on vacations. It's all the things around you—things you see, touch, smell or hear. (*If you taste it, you probably ate it...which is more of a health issue*). You don't have to own them to have them be part of your surroundings and affect your life.

Your surroundings may be rundown and depressing—weighing down your life and making daily existence a struggle. Or your surroundings can be in good condition, comfortable and even beautiful—giving an uplifting energy to your life and helping you be happy with the things you do. You have the ability to make some simple changes in your surroundings which can propel your life forward in a very positive way.

Let's look at some aspects of poor surroundings, then see how these can be transitioned into good surroundings.

When things aren't working right and you get burnt toast in the morning, the shower switches from burning hot to ice cold, your e-mail is messed up *again*, and it takes forever to get your car started, it can ruin your day. The combined effect of fiddling with things like these can cause a mountain of lost time in your life. Time you could be spending having fun, or doing something to make your life better.

Besides lost time, these things can put you in a bad mood. Even if you're normally a very nice person, you can get upset—it happens. And once you're there, you're poorly prepared to deal with the other problems of the day. Things that might normally roll off your back become a big deal, hot words may be exchanged, or you may feel depressed about how lousy things have gotten. Often times it's due to—or made worse by—little things going wrong around you.

What is the effect on your health when your surroundings are too cold, too hot, too wet or too noisy? Poor conditions leave your body weak and make it malfunction (*heat prostration, fainting*), lower your resistance to viruses, or bring on headaches. Even if no major physical problem results, you can have difficulty concentrating or doing physical tasks, and you may be susceptible to making errors, having to do things again.

Something as basic as having a battered, old car or shabby, out-of-style clothes can create an unfavorable impression on people you meet in your career or social life.

If the neighborhood where you live or work has graffiti on the buildings, gunshots are heard at night, and people with bad attitudes follow you down the sidewalk, this can also have an effect on your life. Anxiety and fear can limit what you do, where you go, who you talk to. If this is a situation you find yourself in, you might want to keep an eye open for the chance to move into new surroundings.

At the other end of the spectrum, having good things around you can give an upward push to your life.

What would happen if you were able to replace those things at home and at work that are broken or waste your time? In reality, they probably can't all be replaced at once, but you can make major progress in this direction.

What if that gave you a little more time every day to have fun or do something to improve your life. Would that be useful? I've done it...and wouldn't have it any other way.

How about the hot-water, cold-water showers, messed up e-mail and other things that get you a little angry or upset? Are these things you can fix or get someone else to repair? What if you not only got rid of some irritating things but added something positive—like a coffeemaker that gets your morning cup going before you wake up? What happens if you leave the house with a smile in the morning...do you think your day will go better?

We talked about how your home or place of work could have temperature extremes and other problems. What if they not only didn't have big problems but had something to actually make them more comfortable? What if there was an area rug on that cold tile at home, or better lighting at your place of work? Would fewer colds or headaches improve your performance and your life?

Having all the tools you need doesn't just apply to the workshop or kitchen. The mobile phone has gone from science fiction to virtual life-saver. Educational games like Math Blaster for the personal computer can give children an advantage in school (*my friends Jan and Bob Davidson started that company; if anyone in this field deserves our thanks, they do*). Sometimes having things is not just a status symbol, but can add to your quality of life.

The things we wear influence other people's opinion of us. I'm as guilty as anyone of having something that's really comfortable and wearing it until it falls apart. I found a reasonable compromise by wearing comfortable old favorites around the house, but mixing in new things from time to time when I'm with other people. Don't get me wrong...I like to dress up in a tuxedo once a year for a special evening out, and enjoy looking good. But, like a lot of guys, going shopping for clothes is not something I do often. Maybe you'll have an easier time with this than I did.

I've already mentioned how the money you earn from your career affects your ability to buy things. But your career does much more than that. Many people collect things related to their work: photos with people in their field, awards, trophies, T-shirts. The same is true of their unpaid, avid interest. And they gather things from travel done in pursuit of their career. If your work is conservative or artsy, blue collar or white collar, it affects your taste in clothes, home furnishings, car and much more. Altogether, these things become the image and level of comfort that surround your life.

Your frame of mind also affects the things around you. Some of us have a "rustic, down-home, unpretentious" style. Others opt for "I don't care what condition my things are in, I'm into my art, my career." Still others prefer the "modest, well-kept, other people will like this" style. While others have the "upscale, successful, the best available" style. Some people, with exquisite taste and financial ability, create surroundings so beautiful it takes your breath away. As your frame of mind and desires change, your surroundings sometimes change as well.

In terms of the neighborhood where you live or work, more and more people are making this a priority in their lives. Even when it means a step down in income, Americans have been migrating from cities to rural areas in record numbers over the past ten years. It's not for everyone—but for some people, it's exactly the thing they need to put their life in order.

You have many opportunities to create a more enjoyable environment that helps improve your life. While time and money are always considerations, it's possible to upgrade your surroundings significantly, even if what you have is fairly minimal in the beginning.

This begins with small steps: getting a leafy, potted plant; buying a new article of clothing or an accessory; replacing a small thing that's broken with something that's new, smooth-working and attractive. As these steps continue, more and more of your surroundings are converted into things you really enjoy.

Imagine all the wonderful things you could have around you. Beautiful things. Exciting things. Comfortable things. Pleasing things. They can be yours.

Steps

Having said that, let's identify what you can do to bring the benefits of enjoyable surroundings into your life.

Think of some small **things** you could acquire which would remind people of the word you chose earlier. For now, just look at things related to your surroundings. Jot them here.

Things	____________________________
you	____________________________
could	____________________________
acquire	____________________________

Now think of some things or activities in your life the way it is today, which suggest the **opposite** of that word. Remember we're only addressing your surroundings at this point. Jot those here.

Opposite

of

your

word

Next, think of some **skills** you could acquire, or ongoing **activities** you could do—related to having enjoyable surroundings—which would remind people of the word you chose. Note those here.

Skills

and

activities

Using our example of how this might look with the word **wealthy,** you might have come up with thoughts on the three lists like these

Surroundings   You've still got an old couch in the living room. You could replace it.

You've been going to an average place to get your hair cut or styled. Find someone who's got a great look and start going where they go.

Now go over your three lists above:

Acquire: things you might get

Opposite: things you might fix

Activities: things you might do

Add any new thoughts which occur to you.

As you did earlier, pick **one** thing from the lists which meets these criteria: it's something you could do easily and soon, without too much cost.

Copy that one item here.

Surroundings: ___________________________

All right! Save this step and we'll come back to it.

You're almost done. Just one more to go, then we can start the enjoyable work of bringing these good things into your life.

Peace of Mind

Most of us don't realize the wide-ranging effect peace of mind has on our quality of life…until we don't have it any longer. Sometimes the worries, troubles and stress pile up so much that it seems almost unbearable. It happens often enough that people gave it a name: "hitting bottom." Some people come back up, some don't.

The opposite is also true. Some people hit a "natural high" which fuels their imagination and energy so much they accomplish incredible things and leave others in awe. Occasionally an artist, performer, minister, scientist or athlete reaches such incredible heights, and seems like such a good person, they inspire legions of others.

True? Consider these: Walt Whitman, Tom Cruise, Billy Graham, Albert Einstein, Michael Jordan.

Unfortunately, most of us seem to get stuck at lower levels. Sometimes people are wedged in so low there's a river of difficulties flowing through their life and they become numb. Terrible times seem "normal." Maybe you know someone who lives with an abusive spouse or parent, and seeing it makes you ache. Yet the person involved suffers quietly and seems to accept it as their life.

What are some of the things which, if they could be handled, would make your life much better?

For most of us there are nagging doubts about things that happened in the past—such as the time we did something to hurt the feelings of a friend, family member or sex partner. It still comes back and gives us a twinge of pain once in a while. Or the time we said something out of anger, jealousy or attempted humor that etched pain and hurt on someone's face. Sometimes your conscience is your toughest judge.

That has a strong effect on your peace of mind. You find yourself "walking on egg shells" around some people because of previous problems. You can't sleep some nights. You talk on and on to a friend, trying to unburden yourself over what happened. You wonder if you're a bad person because you do these things. It hangs on you and you can't seem to shake it.

Other things also affect your peace of mind, like the people and things around you. The abusive person is one example. Crime in your neighborhood is another.

Reports of burglaries or killings nearby—on streets where you've walked—can cause real concern. You may be walking down a dark sidewalk at night and find your heart beating faster. You look at each shadowy, approaching figure and wonder if they're going to do something. Even if only a small touch of anxiety happens, it puts a hint of fear in the air that permeates your life. It can restrict your life and keep you from doing things that people in other places take for granted.

Pressures at work can be no less demanding. Sometimes there's too much that needs to get done, not enough people to do it, things go wrong, and someone gets the blame. Performance counts for something, but then there's "politics." People are sometimes fired. If it's you, how well would you take it? What would your family and friends think? These are concerns that cross people's minds.

Your health can be a serious source of worry. As the years roll by, you find your body isn't healing itself as well as it once did. New concerns come up. Friends die from cancer or AIDS. Then from heart attacks. Each year you feel a little more mortal. Some aches don't go away...can that possibly be arthritis so soon? Hair loss. Vision loss. The prospect of dying feels more real. You wonder when it will end. Sometimes you think about it during the day, then it keeps you awake half the night.

And what about the rest of your life? Will you ever accomplish anything lasting? Will anyone care? Is there life after death as some say? Should you be more involved in your religion? Are there other choices? What's the right thing to do?

As it turns out, there are many things you can do. It's a matter of taking charge of your life and starting to work on the things which are really important to you. In fact, you can eventually live life at the higher end of the spectrum.

What would it do for your life if your surroundings were safe and comfortable...if the people you see on the street look forward to meeting you and lend a hand if you need it? You can take a big step in that direction by talking with more of your neighbors. Neighborhood watch groups are great in this respect. I belong to one myself. I meet a lot of people that way—which drastically reduces the number of "strangers" I see when walking at night. Some neighbors ask me to watch their house when they're on vacation, and they do the same in return. If doing things like this seem impossible for you and you still hear gunfire at night, consider moving. But in most cases you can take steps to feel much safer.

How would you feel if your health was getting better, and physical concerns had been erased by reliable tests? What if you hadn't felt this good in years and, instead of cutting back on activities because you're "over the hill," you're taking up a new sport like skiing or sailing? Would that put a different light on your life?

And what if there was something really good happening in the rest of your life so you have something to look forward to with excitement? Getting your life unstuck and making real progress toward the goals in your life can do small miracles for you. And dramatically improve your outlook on life and peace of mind.

Is there an after-life? Many religious and spiritual groups are so certain it's true that there may very well be something to it. But I'm not really in a position to give you spiritual or religious advice here. Talk with people you respect in this area and get their guidance. If you develop an understanding that works for you, it can go a long way toward giving you a calmer and happier view of life.

Achieving more peace of mind helps all the different parts of your life. Not only that, it makes you feel much better. You've probably had an occasion or two when you've felt so good you were radiating good will and happiness to everyone around you. Wouldn't it be great to feel like that every day of your life?

Meditation

If you're interested in peace of mind and relaxation you've almost certainly come across references to meditation, or even tried it. This turns out to be one of several good ways to achieve positive results and is becoming so popular that it's worth mentioning here.

As you probably know, meditation isn't new—it's been practiced for thousands of years in the Far East. But it's relatively new in the Western World.

It didn't really catch on until Transcendental Meditation in the 1960's. A cheerful fellow named Maharishi Mahesh Yogi made meditation an "in" thing among the "flower children" of the day. Four early converts were John, Paul, George and Ringo—also known as The Beatles. They happily inhaled and meditated, and a generation joined them.

That could have been the end of the matter. But several TMers (*as the followers of the Maharishi were known*) went to Harvard professor Herbert Benson and said they believed they could change their blood pressure at will— just by thinking. For whatever reason, the good professor took their dare and conducted a formal study. He demonstrated with medical correctness that the claim was true. Heart rate, respiratory rate and high blood pressure were all reduced very significantly by meditation.

His book, *The Relaxation Response,* sold millions of copies, and is still in bookstores now.

Over the years, meditation groups and classes have multiplied in every part of the United States and around the world. This made the ground fertile for other ideas and concepts from the Far East, and prepared the way for popular works by people like Deepak Chopra.

A Personal Journey

Have you ever been going along in your everyday life when something unexpected happens and sends you in completely new direction? It may already have happened to you once or twice. It's amazing.

It happened to me.

After getting caught up in the whirlwind of hectic modern life—school, marriage, work, divorce, early "success" and a six figure income—I was very unhappy.

That's when a small miracle happened.

A friend made me an offer I couldn't refuse. Literally. He was my boss.

As president, he decided he and the other officers would go, one by one, to a week-long "leadership workshop." It sounded like one of those touchy-feely things.

I told him, "Thanks anyway, but. . . ."

My boss countered, "You like getting that paycheck?"

The silver-tongued fox had me there. So I gave in. Even so, I was the last to go.

He told me to go to the workshop, say anything I wanted and not worry, because I wouldn't know anyone in the group and would never see them again. He lied. A year later our group arranged a reunion, flying in from all over the country just to see each other again and re-live the experience. What happened?

I arrived in North Carolina on the first day of the workshop, at a rural retreat where the program would be held, and settled in for a week of who-knows-what. It began with classroom work. I started to relax. I could handle this.

The next day we showed up for the self-awareness part of the workshop. Big room. Carpeted floor. No chairs. We were told to sit on the floor in a circle. Oh damn...

The instructor started with a question. "How many of you feel like you're normal?"

Everyone put up their hand except yours truly. I wasn't sure what he meant by normal, but had never been accused of that so I let it ride.

He quoted a brief definition:

Normal human beings are happy and joyous in living;
Are excited, stimulated, and satisfied by what they do;
Are never bored, and do not let boring persons or situations impose themselves persistently.
They give and find love and pleasure in rela-tionships

> *And are openly and realistically assertive in dealing*
> *with their environment.*
> *They suffer unavoidable pain and loss with*
> *minimum necessary attention*
> *And never create unnecessary pain or trouble for*
> *themselves or others.*
> *They are alert and alive in their entire being,*
> *In touch with and feeling to be a part of their sur-*
> *rounding world,*
> *Eating and enjoying what they need,*
> *Needing what they eat,*
> *Liking and caring for their bodies as integral parts of*
> *their being.*
> *Above all, through learning from the past and*
> *looking to the future, a normal human being*
> *always lives in the here and now.*[1]

"That's the way you were when you were born," he said. "Now look how messed up you are!"

We all laughed. Especially me. I could really identify with that.

Day after day we went into all kinds of things about our lives. Things I'd never thought about. Door after door was unlocked (*so to speak*) and I went through at my own pace, in my own way. It was amazing.

After one particular session, some big pieces fell into place. It was an incredible feeling. I stumbled outside and walked a ways in the beautiful green countryside. Everything seemed crystal clear, as though I had never seen it before. I sat under a pine tree. Every emerald needle on the nearest bough stood out in golden sunlight.

---

1. James N. Farr., **Experiencing Aliveness** (*see bibliography*)

A small striped bee landed on a purple wildflower. He wasn't afraid of me and I wasn't afraid of him. I leaned closer. He gathered pollen from the flower onto his back legs, then lifted up and took off in a straight line, probably back to his hive.

I got up and wandered back to my own group, late for lunch but not caring.

I'd started a new journey on which other breakthroughs would come that were no less spectacular.

The journey took me to many places. Other workshops. Religious groups. University libraries. Health groups. Career development programs. Environmental groups. Social groups. Seven years later, the LifeCycle was born.

As you go forward, I hope your journey of discovery will turn out to be as enjoyable as mine continues to be.

Steps

To begin this phase of your journey, consider what you can do to bring benefits from peace of mind into your life.

Think of some small **things** you could acquire which would remind people of the word you chose earlier. For now, just look at things related to relaxation and peace of mind. Jot them here.

Things

you

could

acquire

Now think of some things or activities in your life the way it is today, which suggest the **opposite** of that word. Remember we're only addressing your peace of mind at this point. Jot those here.

Opposite

of

your

word

Next, think of some **skills** you could acquire, or ongoing **activities** you could do—related to having peace of mind—which would remind people of the word you chose. Note those here.

Skills ________________________________

and   ________________________________

activities ________   ________________

Following up on our example of how this might look with the word **wealthy,** you might have come up with thoughts on the three lists like these.

Peace of Mind   Your vacations tend to be repeated visits to relatives. You could do one trip to Hawaii or Bermuda, and bring back mementos for your home and workplace.

Your work and life tend to be stressful. You could sign up for a weekend stress reduction program at a local spa.

Now go over your three lists above:

Acquire: things you might get

Opposite: things you might fix

Activities: things you might do

Add any new thoughts which occur to you.

As before, pick **one** thing from the lists which meets these criteria: it's something you could do easily and soon, without too much cost.

Copy that one item here.

Peace of Mind:

That's it! Now you have all the things you need to start bringing into your life all the benefits you've identified. Let's go!

Getting Your Life Going

New concepts and ideas are only of value if you put them to work in your life and make good things happen. It's time to take those steps and get your life going.

Let's start by gathering the necessary ingredients. Copy the following things from the six previous sections.

Write your key word here—the one that would make you feel good if you were considered exceptional in this way.

____

At the top of the next page copy the one item you identified at the end of each of the previous sections—the thing which you could do easily and soon, without too much cost.

		TARGET	DONE	TOLD
Health			☐	☐
Relationships			☐	☐
Career			☐	☐
Surroundings			☐	☐
Peace of mind			☐	☐

Now pick the item from this list which seems to be the easiest, quickest, or least expensive to do. If two are about equal, flip a coin. Pick one and write a "1" in front of it. This is the first step you're going to take to make your life better.

Set a target date for finishing this item. Can you complete it this week? Pick the earliest reasonable date and write it on the "Target" line for that item.

This is the moment your life begins to get better.

Start work on that item no later than today or tomorrow. If your life is important to you, just do it. Even if it's only making telephone calls to get information. Stay on it until it's done. If you have to put something else off to do this, it's worth it. This is an adventure. The results are hard to describe...you'll experience them soon.

When it's done, check off the "Done" box.

One more step on this item, and it's very important. Show it to someone or tell them about it. It's not bragging. It's something you've done and you're letting a friend know. Friends like to know these things. This step is essential because things you share with others or tell them about become "real." Take my word for it, this makes a difference.

Congratulations! One item done!

Check off the "Told" box and enjoy what you've accomplished. Feels good, doesn't it?

That's one down. The LifeCycle process is well under way. There are more rewards ahead

Pick one of the remaining four items.

Write the number "2" in front of it.

Set a target date for it.

Jump on it and do it.

Tell someone.

Catch your breath and enjoy.

Then do the next one.

Something unusual will start to happen. You'll notice as you do the second and third items that they are beginning to interact. The benefit from one starts to help the others.

After you do the third one, catch your breath, then keep going. You need to finish the last two to get the full effect.

Finished all five? Yes!

You've completed the first *full cycle* of improvement in your life.

That's quite an accomplishment. And you're now in a position to share your accomplishments with others.

Take a few quiet minutes by yourself to consider the small journey you've taken. Think back to how things were before you started the LifeCycle process. Have you gotten any insights? Did the five items you accomplished give you a little more of what you want most in life? Did it touch the different parts of your life, and prepare you to go on and have even more of what you want? How do you feel about it?

It's important to write down your thoughts about what you experienced. This simple act helps you keep the benefits active in your life. It's a success, you really accomplished something. Jot your thoughts here.

Success Story

Mark one: ☐ To encourage other people to make improvements to their lives, this story can be shared with others

☐ Don't share it with others.

Your Name

Date

Real-life experiences like yours can be inspirational to other people and help them get the energy to make improvements in their lives. Share your story with them by sending it to me in care of: Sierra Sunrise, 14622 Ventura Blvd., PMB 800, Sherman Oaks, CA 91403.

If you've been reading along and haven't started the LifeCycle process yet: get your word, find your first item and get started. A better, happier life is waiting for you.

Enjoy!

Getting Your Life Going
Part 2

F inishing a full cycle of the LifeCycle process is a real accomplishment! Let's take a look at what you've achieved and where you go from here.

You've already taken five steps—one in each of the five parts of your life. This is important for several reasons. I suggested you start with small steps so you could jump right on it and do them in a reasonable amount of time. You've done that. And it's important you keep moving ahead this way.

Remember the example I used earlier about the tall, stone tower which at first seems impossible to climb? The secret, of course, is to look for the small steps. Things you **can** do. And do them. One small step at a time up the stairs, higher and higher, until you reach the top.

And that special word you selected? It's something worth having, something that can make you stand out among other people. And it moves you closed to what you want most in life.

The fun part comes next.

Something truly remarkable happened when you were taking a small step forward in all five parts of your life. If you do one step and get one "benefit," you'd think taking five steps would give you five "benefits." It doesn't. You get much more.

Remember the LifeCycle connections between the different parts of your life? You literally start to see them and feel them as you work through the five items in the full cycle. In completing your first full cycle, did one of the steps prove useful to you in doing one of the others? Did one of the four non-relationship items help your relationship with someone? Did one of the four non-surroundings items do something to help your surroundings?

The best is yet to come.

To get it, do another cycle. Why? Because the steps you take from now on will benefit from all the steps you've already completed. Eventually it gets to be like popcorn going off—good things happen all around you. In scientific terms this is called a critical mass. When you get enough good things going for you they take on a life of their own and carry you forward, like the flow of a river that's running in the direction you want to go. Eventually you're able to do things that seemed almost unachievable a short while ago.

Let me show you how it works. Remember the "wealthy" example I used earlier? A number of steps were identified which could get a person started. Quite honestly, doing one full cycle will not make you wealthy.

It does, however, move you in the right direction. It gets you started and gives you the building blocks to go farther: more of the image of wealth, more contact with people who have wealth, more of the things which make you a little more like "us" (*wealthy*) instead of "them" (*not wealthy*), and which give you a little more understanding of investment and return. You start to see the small amount of time and money you invest in each item of the cycle is giving you something of value in return—you're starting to accumulate things of value in your life.

When does it become real wealth? When you've talked extensively with wealthy people about their investments and returns, when you've met their advisors and investors, and when you've done cycles of small investments with your own money to give you the feel and understanding of what it takes to be successful at a higher level. Then you'll be a player—with knowledge, contacts and money to invest (*it's been growing slowly while you've been learning*). It doesn't happen suddenly. You start down the road, keep doing small cycles, and eventually you're there.

How do you get the energy to do the next full cycle? Easy. Teamwork.

Teamwork

Get yourself a partner in this great game. It doesn't have to be your partner-for-life...a good friend will do just fine. It can be anyone who wants to take a shot at improving their life. This last part is very important. They have to be a participant, not an observer. They have to want something to be better in their life and be very interested, along with you, in doing this.

Go through the whole process together. If only one of you has read this book, the other one needs to start there. You can lend them your copy of the book—**there's a full set of forms in the back for them to use.** But it's even better if you take them to get their own book. Or give them one—what are friends for? (*And part of your payback is that they're going to be helping you with your next cycle.*) It's better if you each have your own copy to refer to as you go through this energizing journey.

Both of you should read as far as the section, "What Would You Like To Have?" Then **separately** fill in the questionnaire. For you, it may simply be an update of what you've already done. Compare the results, if you like, only after both of you finish that section. This is important.

Why? Because the benefit of doing the LifeCycle with someone else doesn't come from copying their answers or having them follow yours. It comes from sharing with someone the energy and good feeling of really starting to get somewhere in life. It's having someone be excited when you finish another step. Someone who just can't wait to tell you about the step they completed. The energy it gives you is great, and will carry you right through the next cycle.

The benefits you get are for you. Your desires, your path, your steps to get there.

Encourage your teammate to find their desires, their path, their steps. The better they feel about what they're doing, the more energy it gives you—it propels you both forward.

When both of you have done the reading and questionnaires up to and including "Getting Your Life Going," you're ready for the fun part. With five items in front of each of you (*five new ones for you*), pick your first one and set a target date. Your partner should do the same. Tell each other what you picked and what you're going to do about it. Such as: join a gym to get more exercise. They may suggest you consider Tae Kwon Do. You say you're not sure, but you think you had that for lunch. They explain it's a real workout and more interesting than a weight room. Maybe you pass on that, but accept their offer to get you into their gym at half price. Be sure to ask what they picked, and maybe offer to return the favor they did for you. It's teamwork.

A short while later comes an important milestone: you finish your first item and tell them about it. Congratulations are in order! A few days later they finish and you get to enjoy their success!

Very important—don't wait for your partner to make progress. As you finish one item, start the next. Maybe gently prod your partner, kid them or encourage them, but keep your own items going. They may be a slow starter but a fast finisher. Don't stop until your full cycle is done. Set a good example, show them how to do it.

The same holds true if the roles are reversed. Your partner might zip right through the first item while you're only halfway there. It's not a big deal. As long as you're making progress, that's what counts. You'll get there, and it won't take much longer. That's why we pick small steps. Your partner will be there for you when you finish and it will be great.

When both of you have finished all five steps and have a full cycle to your credit, do the right thing. Celebrate! Not because you want to feel good and have fun (*?!*) but because you have to. It's a duty! Your partner deserves a good night out; maybe you can have dinner together. Enjoy!

Completing a full cycle with someone is very significant. It's a shared experience you'll probably remember for a long time. They will too. And your life is that much better for having done it.

Mentor

After you've done a full cycle by yourself or with a partner, there's something else you can do for a different flavor and even more satisfaction. Get someone <u>new</u> involved in the process. You can be a mentor to them and lead the way.

There are obvious benefits to them. They get to be with someone who's been through it and can guide them to a successful and happy completion.

There are also major benefits for you. The first happens right away. There's something great about having other people look up to you for your knowledge and experience. And if you've been through the LifeCycle process already, you really do have something of value. Their respect is well earned.

The other benefit to you comes throughout the time you spend with them. Sure, you're making good personal progress. But after many small victories at doing anything, we sometimes develop the "been there" attitude. It's natural. There's no better tonic than to go through the process with someone who's never done it. Their wide-eyed excitement may seem a little overdone to an experienced person like yourself, but it's also contagious. Your knowledge will carry them through. Their energy will carry you through. It's a great relationship. And it's fun to do it this way.

Groups

If you did the previous cycle with a partner, both of you could become mentors on the next cycle. Find two new people who would like to give the LifeCycle a try. Pair up so each new person has one mentor. That person is their main guide through the journey. But all four of you can help each other and give encouragement throughout the cycle. Again—gently prod the others who are lagging, but don't wait for them. Go ahead and finish. When all of you are done, super celebrate!

If you've done at least one full cycle with someone and really want to have a big effect on the world around you, consider setting up a LifeCycle group. You already have two members when you start, and it grows fairly quickly. To do it, just send an e-mail or letter to me at <u>LifeCycle@LifeOnNet.org</u> or Sierra Sunrise, 14622 Ventura Blvd., PMB 800, Sherman Oaks, CA 91403. Or fax it to (818) 386-9102. Include a success story on your full cycle. You'll receive in the mail a package of clean forms, more information on the LifeCycle, and some suggestions on how to attract interested people to join you.

In return I'd like to hear how you're doing, and what good things are happening in your life. And I may refer some local media people to you for human interest stories. Everyone likes to hear about successes. Why not yours?

> *P.S.—visit our website at **www.LifeOnNet.org**
> and see what people are doing with LifeCycle*

When It Comes Together

I've always been intrigued by the people who wrote their name large on the course of history. Especially those who didn't gain their position of enormous respect by inheritance or fighting battles.

That must have been sitting in the back of my mind when I came across the LifeCycle, because another breakthrough occurred. The source of those people's success became much clearer. They each seem to have worked out a concept similar to the LifeCycle to guide themselves.

You've already seen the example of Socrates. He earned his living doing what he loved to do: talking with influential people about intriguing concepts in life and receiving their patronage in return. Clearly he achieved as high a level as is possible in his career and relationships (*though jealousy over his success eventually cost him his life—those were not tolerant times*). He lived to be seventy in robust good health, enjoyed a comfortable lifestyle in art-filled Athens, was remarkably witty, relaxed and insightful. So he also ranks at the highest levels in healthy body, surroundings and peace of mind. Altogether, he lived a complete life. His success in each area propelled the other areas higher until the upward spiral raised him far above the other people of his day.

Leonardo da Vinci loomed almost as large as the towering statues of his time. He was described as "a man both of beauty and grace and of great physical strength. His mind also was remarkable...he was interested in and more or less an adept at almost every branch of art, science and philosophy. He was something of a humanist and musician and also had a mechanical turn of mind. Some of the sketches in his notebooks seem to forecast modern inventions." [1]

The image of Leonardo was of someone who pursued his interests, was handsomely rewarded, lived a hale and hearty life to age 67 in beautiful Florence, Italy, possessed clear vision and a clear mind, and was sought-after by others. Again, a person who lived a complete life.

Benjamin Franklin was as colorful as he was influential in his day. Successful in business early in life, he was able to pursue whatever endeavors interested him, and there were many. Besides being one of the founders of the United States, he was an avid inventor, scientist, author and diplomat. Charming and witty, he dazzled influential people in Europe as well as America. Franklin lived to be 84, enjoying life to the fullest.

---

1. Lynn Thorndike, **History of Medieval Europe** (*see bibliography*)

Albert Einstein was known primarily as the physicist who invented the theory of relativity. But he also had a sly sense of humor and actively pursued his interests in international affairs, thinking nothing of calling on some of the greatest people of his time to express his views. His relationships were such that those people listened, and even sought his advice. He lived to 76, still active and teaching.

Mother Teresa was an Albanian nun who founded a religious order dedicated to aiding the poor. In 1979 she won the Nobel peace prize for her work in the slums of Calcutta. Her personal surroundings were very modest, but she seemed to revel in her life and the fact that she could touch the hearts of so many people. She lived to 87 years of age.

Many people achieve fame in one of the five areas of life: a great athlete, a famous actor, an elected official, a religious leader, a champion of nature. But most of them never achieve a complete life. Lacking one or more of the other essential areas, many of them die depressed, bitter or reclusive.

The few who achieve success in all five areas tend to rise above others, garner ongoing respect, and enjoy life for all their years.

You don't have to be famous to enjoy a good life. But if you build up all five areas of your life, you can enjoy what you have to the fullest.

A Final Word

There is an ancient Chinese saying attributed to Lao Tzu which translates as, "A trip of a thousand miles begins with a single step." More recent times added, "The whole is greater than the sum of its parts." The list of insights go on and on. In other words, all the pieces of the LifeCycle have always been there.

It's not like I've discovered the genius of life that no one else ever saw.

It's just that I finally understand it.

Now, I hope you do too.

All net proceeds from the publication of *LifeCycle* are donated to LifeWorks Institute.

LifeWorks Institute is a nonprofit, public service organization dedicated to helping people improve their lives. It does this by sponsoring the development and publication of materials on life improvement. These materials and related services are provided free of charge to schools and community organizations.

Holistic View of the World

While each of us draws on all the parts of our life whenever we create something new—whether as an artist, a carpenter or social leader—there is always something which is particularly important. For the creation of the LifeCycle, that important thing was the holistic view of the world.

If you're curious to peek behind the scenes and learn more about the foundation on which the LifeCycle is built, this material will be an eye-opening experience for you. It was for me.

What is the true meaning of "holistic"? Many people assume it's another name for alternative medicine, but we see here it's much more than that.

I originally thought "holistic" must be an ancient word with roots in the Far East, because of the many ancient traditions in India and China which refer to a larger view of life. As it turns out, it has a different source.

I was amazed to discover the holistic approach to life sprang from the work of one man. And was published in a single book in 1926. The person was Jan Christiaan Smuts (*pronounced "smoots"—as in "boots"*). The book was **Holism and Evolution**. He created the word "holistic" to describe his concept.

We come to understand Holism as a universal force in nature which works toward the creation of wholes, causing them to be successful and thrive. This view produces valuable insights into life, science and nature.

The content of **Holism** is so rich in thought and wide in application that it deserves to be read by itself.

For the full text, see the newly re-issued

Holism and Evolution *by Jan Christiaan Smuts,*

edited by Sanford Holst.

Sierra Sunrise Books. ISBN 1-887263-14-4

To give you the essential ideas and thoughts behind the holistic view of the world, I've identified highlights of the book and shown them on the following pages.

The Author of Holism and Evolution

Jan Christiaan Smuts was no less remarkable than his uplifting concepts and inspiring ideas. Educated at Cambridge in England just before the year 1900, he had an elegant turn of phrase and encyclopedic knowledge which seemed to belong to a gracious age. Yet his life was anything but calm and gentle. Growing up in South Africa during the Boer War, he served a term as Prime Minister of his country. At leisure after public duty, he put pen to paper and wrote *Holism and Evolution*, pouring out the thoughts, dreams and experiences of a full and colorful life.

Yet his days on the world stage were not over. Re-elected as Prime Minister, he presided over a country struggling with a new concept called apartheid—the forced separation of blacks and whites. He opposed that policy and stood his ground under relentless attack. Forced from office, he retired once more to private life. No other South African Prime Minister would oppose apartheid until Nelson Mandela.

The following are some of the cornerstones of life—dreams, principles, strength, wholeness and a calm view of life which survives turbulence in the world around us and revels in the beauty of nature.

Holism and Evolution

These quotes reveal the holistic approach to life in the actual words first used to describe it. Hopefully this will let you see as well as feel the original vision. The quotes are condensed slightly to convey the key ideas in as readable a manner as possible.

PREFACE

"This work deals with our primary concepts of matter, life, mind and personality...and discusses some of the problems of evolution from this new point of view.

"It is my belief that Holism and the holistic point of view will prove important in their bearings on some of the main problems of science and philosophy, ethics, art and allied subjects."

FUNDAMENTAL CONCEPTS

"In spite of the great advances which have been made in knowledge, some fundamental gaps still remain: matter, life and mind still remain utterly disparate phenomena. Yet the concepts of all three arise in experience, and in the human all three meet and apparently intermingle.

"Our physical science ought to provide the solvent for our idea of hard impenetrable inert **matter**.

"Our biological science should dispel the vagueness of the concept of **life**, and replace it by a more definite meaningful concept, which will yet not depend on purely material or physical elements.

"**Mind** again, which is closest to us in experience, becomes farthest from us in exact thought. The concepts in which we envisage it are so vague and nebulous, compared with the hard and rigid contours of our concepts of matter, that the two appear poles asunder.

"Matter, life and mind are, so to speak, the original alphabet of knowledge, the original nuclei of all experience, thought, and speculation.

"In Darwin's theory of Descent...Natural Selection is usually but erroneously taken to be a purely mechanical factor.

"There is, however one form of Selection which cannot be thus indiscriminately dealt with. It arises not only from organic causes, but still more narrowly and quite indisputably from physical or mental causes. Darwin called it Sexual Selection.

"It is clear that the real motive power of this form of selection is mostly biological and psychical. The female is excited and attracted by superior fighting force or superior artistic endowments among males competing for her favour.

"The science of the nineteenth century was like its philosophy, its morals and its civilisation in general, distinguished by a certain hardness, primness and precise limitation and demarcation of ideas.

"Concepts were in logic as well as in science narrowed down to their most luminous points, and the rest of their contents treated as non-existent. Situations were not envisaged as a whole of clear and vague obscure elements alike, but were analyzed merely into their clear, outstanding luminous points.

"We have to return to the fluidity and plasticity of nature and experience in order to find the concepts of reality. When we do this we find that round every luminous point in experience there is a gradual shading off into haziness and obscurity.

"Conceive of a cause as a centre with a zone of activity or influence surrounding it and shading gradually off into indefiniteness. Next conceive of an effect as similarly surrounded. It is easy in that way to understand their interaction, and to see that cause and effect are interlocked, and embrace and influence each other through the interpenetration of their two fields.

"In fact the conception of Field of force which has become customary in Electro-Magnetism is only a special case of phenomenon which is quite universal in the realms of thought and reality alike."

GENERAL CONCEPT OF HOLISM

"The close approach to each other of the concepts of matter, life and mind, and their partial overflow of each other's domain, raises the further question whether back of them there is not a fundamental principle of which they are the progressive outcome.

"Both matter and life consist of unit structures whose ordered grouping produces natural wholes which we call bodies or organisms. This character of "wholeness" meets us everywhere and points to something fundamental in the universe. Holism (*from* $o\lambda os$ = *whole*) is the term here coined for this fundamental factor operative towards the creation of wholes in the universe. Its character is both general and specific or concrete, and it satisfies our double requirement for a natural evolutionary starting-point.

"Wholes are not mere artificial constructions of thought; they point to something real in the universe, and Holism is a real operative factor, a *vera causa*. There is behind Evolution no mere vague creative impulse or *Elan vital*, but something quite definite and specific in its operation, and thus productive of the real concrete character of cosmic Evolution.

"The idea of wholes and wholeness should therefore not be confined to the biological domain; it covers both inorganic substances and the highest manifestations of the human spirit.

"Taking a plant or animal as a type of a whole, we notice the fundamental holistic characters as a unity of parts which is so close and intense as to be more than the sum of its parts; which not only gives a particular conformation or structure to the parts but so relates and determines them in their synthesis that their functions are altered.

"The synthesis affects and determines the parts, so that they function towards the "whole"; and the whole and the parts therefore reciprocally influence and determine each other, and appear more or less to merge their individual characters: the whole is in the parts and the parts are in the whole, and this synthesis of whole and parts is reflected in the holistic character of the functions of the parts as well of the whole.

"There is a progressive grading of this holistic synthesis in Nature, so that we pass from

(a) mere physical mixtures, where the structure is almost negligible, and the parts largely preserve their separate characters and activities or functions, to

(b) chemical compounds, where the structure is more synthetic and the activities and functions of the parts are strongly influenced by the new structure and can only with difficulty be traced to the individual parts; and, again, to

(c) organisms, where a still more intense synthesis of elements has been effected, which impresses the parts or organs far more intimately with a unified character, and a system of central control, regulation and co-ordination of all the parts and organs arises; and from organism, again on to

(d) minds or psychical organs, where the Central Control acquires consciousness and a freedom a creative power of the most far-reaching character; and finally to

(e) Personality [the Person], which is the highest, most evolved whole among the structures of the universe, and becomes a new orientative, originative centre of reality.

"All through this progressive series the character of wholeness deepens; Holism is not only creative but self-creative, and its final structures are far more holistic than its initial structures. Natural wholes are always composed of parts; in fact the whole is not something additional to the parts, but is just the parts in their synthesis, which may be physico-chemical or organic or psychical or personal. As Holism is a process of creative synthesis, the resulting wholes are not static but dynamic, evolutionary, creative.

"Hence Evolution has an ever-deepening inward spiritual holistic character; and the wholes of Evolution and the evolutionary process itself can only be understood in reference to this fundamental character of wholeness. This is a universe of whole-making. The explanation of Nature can therefore not be purely mechanical; and the mechanistic concept of Nature has its place and justification only in the wider setting of Holism."

FUNCTIONS AND CATEGORIES

"The most important result of the idea of the whole is, however, the appearance of the concept of Creativeness. It is the synthesis involved in the concept of the whole which is the source of creativeness in Nature. Nature is creative, Evolution is creative, just in proportion as it consists of wholes which bring about new structural groupings and syntheses.

"Thus arise the physical, chemical, organic, psychical and personal categories, which are all expressive of holistic activity at its various levels.

But more; as we proceed upward in the course of Evolution we find....Love, Beauty, Goodness, Truth: they are all of the whole....Holism not only prescribes the law in the world of structures, forms and organisms; It is the very ground and principle of the ideal world of the spirit....Its creativeness will nowhere be found more fruitful than in that last and highest reach of its evolution."

DARWINISM AND HOLISM

"The whole of Darwinian theory is summarized in the last sentences of the *Origin of Species* with a simplicity and beauty of statement worthy of the simple but profound genius of the Master, and they raise before us in a few touches the great Darwinian vision. They have often been quoted, but will bear re-quotation here, and for all time:

It is interesting to contemplate a tangled bank, clothed with many plants of many kinds, with birds singing on the bushes, with various insects flitting about, and with worms crawling through the damp earth, and to reflect that these elaborately constructed forms, so different from each other, and dependent upon each other in so complex a manner, have all been produced by laws acting around us. These laws, taken in the largest sense, being Growth with Reproduction; Inheritance which is almost implied by reproduction; Variability from the indirect and direct action of the conditions of life, and from use and disuse; a Ratio of Increase so high as to lead to a struggle for life, and as a consequence to Natural Selection, entailing Divergence of Character and the extinction of less-improved forms. Thus, from the war of Nature, from famine and death, the most exalted object which we are capable of conceiving, namely, the production of the higher animals, directly follows. There is grandeur in this view of life, with its several powers, having been originally breathed by the Creator into a few forms or into one; and that, whilst this planet has gone cycling on according to the fixed law of gravity, from so simple a beginning endless forms most beautiful and most wonderful have been and are being evolved."

MIND AS AN ORGAN OF WHOLES

"Mind is, after the atom and the cell, the third great fundamental structure of Holism. It is not itself a real whole, but a holistic structure.

"Mind springs from two roots. In the first place, it is a continuation, on a much higher plane, of the system of organic regulation and co-ordination which characterises Holism in organisms.

"In the second place, Mind is a development of an 'individual' aspect of Holism which already plays a subordinate part in organisms. In man it pushes to the front as conscious individuality or the Self of the Personality.

"Mind thus through its power of experience and knowledge comes to master is own conditions of life, to secure freedom and to control the regulative system into which it has been born. Freedom, plasticity, creativeness become the keynotes of the new order of Mind.

"Mind forms 'purposes' which envisage future situations in experience and make the future an operative factor in the present. Purpose marks the liberation of Mind from the domination of circumstances and indicates its free creative activity, away from the trammels of the present and the past. Through purpose Mind finally escapes from the house of bondage in to the free realm of its own sovereignty.

"Consciousness as it develops splits up the indefinite mass of experience into two definite aspects: the self or Subject, which is conscious or attending, the Object, which it attends to or is conscious of. 'The Subject—conscious of—an Object' is thus a general formula for all experience of a mental character.

"**Mind-and-Body** is but a particular form of the general Subject-Object situation. They are not independents, they are interdependents.

"Mind has made all the difference to the later and latest stages of Evolution. Without Mind the organic and regulative process of the universe, vast and magnificent in any case, would have been at best but a tame affair. The universe would have moved forward, as it were in a dream, with an unearthly regularity and majesty of movement. Its process would have become ever more complicated and ever more frictionless, as of some sublime animated machine, great beyond all power of conception. All elements of discord and disharmony would have passed away from its vast cosmic routine. But it would have gone on sublimely unconscious of itself. It would have no soul or souls; it would have harboured no passionate exaltations; no poignant regrets or bitter sorrows would have disturbed its profound peace. For it neither the great lights nor the deep shadows.

"Truth, Beauty and Goodness would have been there, but unknown, unseen, unloved. They would have been cold and passionless like the distant stars, and would never have become the great ideals thrilling and inspiring men and women to deathless action. Love would have been there, but not the immortal emotion which mortals call by that name.

"To the music of the universe there has thus been added a new note, as of laughter and tears, a new undertone of the human, which transforms and enriches all the rest. It is no longer a song of the Golden Reign of the Elder Gods, but of the intertwining of the Cosmos with human Destiny, of the suffering which has become consecrated and illuminated by the great visions, of the magic power of knowledge to work out new enchantments to break the dumb routine, to set the captive spirit free, and to blaze new paths to the immortal Goal.

"Mind has thus added an infinity of light and shade and colour, of inward character and conscious content to the great process in and from which it has emerged.

"Let us dwell for a moment on this new power and mastery which Mind has brought on the scene. Knowledge is power, and it is unnecessary for us here to trace in detail the steps by which the present power and mastery of Science over material conditions have been acquired. Life below the mental level strengthens the innate capacity to react to external influences of a harmful or beneficial nature by various movements which lead successively to the tropisms, reflexes and automatisms of the lower organisms. When Mind appears as an active factor, this power of regulating movements is greatly enlarged and intensified, until we see the sureness and delicacy of the instinctive reactions which characterise all Mind in its subconscious levels.

"It is, however, when consciousness appears that an immense accession to this power of control is brought about. Consciousness, as we have seen, is a power of illuminating objects in the field of experience. The organism through this power of illumination can gradually arrive at a fair knowledge of its surroundings in so far as they are harmful or beneficial to it. Its power of selection is thus more surely guided, and it learns to know accurately and easily what to avoid and what to welcome.

"In the exercise of its free and unhampered right of self-determination, Mind on the human level proceeds to create to a large extent the appropriate conditions for its own development.

"In the organic sphere we saw the individual adapting itself or being adapted to the environment as the imperative condition of its survival. Here we see the environment being more and more adapted to the individual.

"In Mind there is a central illuminated area, the area of full consciousness, which is directly open to inspection and observation. Taking this area as the central structure of Mind, the 'field' of Mind then comes to mean that area of its functions and activities which falls below the 'threshold' of consciousness, which remains unilluminated and dark, which cannot, therefore, be known by direct inspection and which, as in the cases of the other fields, can only be ascertained by its indirect effects.

"The activities of Mind below the level of consciousness are most important for Mind as a whole. It is in this subconscious area or field of its activities that Mind especially feels the pressure of the past.

"The contribution of the past is twofold. In the first place there is the experience of the past in the individual life which has fallen into the background of the Mind and is no longer directly remembered. Yet this experience, as is well known, has a most powerful influence on the conscious present of the experiencing subject. Even the unre-membered past experience is not dead, but alive and active below the level of consciousness. In the debating chamber of the present it may not speak, but it *votes*, and its silent vote is often decisive. Mind does not work in water-tight compartments, its past experience is integral with its present action.

"Memory, the great basic bond of individuality, binding together and fusing all the past phases and expe-rience of the individual with the present into one unique whole which is himself, operates below as well as above the level of consciousness; essentially it forgets nothing and leaves behind nothing of the past. Remembered or unremembered, the past exerts its full force on the present experience.

"The most significant element, however, in the 'field' of Mind concerns the future, and makes the future an operative factor in the present mental activity. Mind does this through purpose; purpose is the function of Mind by which it contemplates some future desired end and makes the idea of this end exert its full force in the present. Thus I form a purpose to go on a hunting expe-dition for my next holiday, and this purpose forms a complex synthesis and sets going a whole series of plans and actions all intended to give effect to the purpose.

"Thus in purpose the future as an object in my mind becomes operative in the present and sets going and controls a long train of acts leading up to the execution of the purpose. The conscious purpose, the end as deliberately envisaged and intended, falls, of course, within the conscious inner area of Mind; but numerous subsidiary elements in the plan would operate subconsciously and thus affect on the field of Mind.

"It will be noticed that purpose or purposive activity involves much more than merely the influence of the future on the present. Purpose is the most complete proof of the freedom and creative power of the mind in respect of its material and other conditions, of its power to create its own conditions and to bring about its own situations for its own free activities.

"My purposive action is action which I have myself planned, which is not impressed on me or dictated to me by external necessity, and for the performance of which I take my own self-chosen measures. Through purpose the mind becomes at last master in its own house, with the power to carry out its own wishes and shape its own course, uninfluenced by the conditions of the environment.

"Again, purposive activity is peculiarly holistic. Elements both of the actual past and of anticipated future experience are fused with the present experience into one individual act, which as a conscious object of the mind dominates the entire situation within the purview of the purpose or plan. It involves not only sensations and perceptions, but also concepts of a complex character, feelings and desires in respect of the end desired, and volitions in respect of the act intended; and all these elements are fused and blended into one unique purpose, which is then put into action or execution. Purpose in thus probably the highest, most complex manifestation of the free, creative, holistic activity of Mind. Purpose is the door through which Mind finally escapes from the house of bondage and enters the free realm of its own sovereignty."

PERSONALITY AS A WHOLE

"Human Personality [a Person] takes up into itself all that has gone before in the cosmic evolution....It is not only mental or spiritual but also organic and material.

"The most characteristic and certainly the most important constituent of Personality is Mind.

"The vast and almost overshadowing importance of the mental or spiritual factor must, however, not blind us to the significance of the other factors, which constitute the body or the physical organism of the human person. These physical organic factors are not only essential, but they also contribute most important features to the human Personality. The human Personality as disembodied spirit and devoid of its physical organism would indeed be something utterly different from what it is. Flesh and blood may not be as important as the soul in the total human make-up, but they are essential and they bring something into the pool which is most vital and precious.

"And the body as transfigured by spirit in man is worthy to be the foundation of the most noble and exalted human Personality. The contempt for the body, the conventional degradation of the body do not spring from a true view of human nature.

"The natural and proper tendency is to look upon the body as clean and wholesome, to rejoice in it as something good and beautiful, to make it twin-sister of the spirit and the embodiment of joyousness and wholesome pleasure. That view of the body finds characteristic expression in Greek literature. It may be a pagan view, but in reality it is the human and true view. It led to respect and reverence for the body, and the culture of the body as a worthy companion of the spirit. This natural and wholesome attitude towards the body was poisoned by the morbid, diseased, religious spirit of a later time which heaped contempt and degradation on the body.

"Science is building up a new world-attitude, a new attitude towards Nature and all things natural, which is totally at variance with this morbid and unnatural condemnation of the flesh. The scientific attitude is impartial and objective and leads to the view of Nature as clean, wholesome and worthy of the respect which is due to all natural facts. Thus a new spirit of respect and reverence for natural things and processes is arising, and not least for the human body—a spirit which is far deeper and better founded than the old happy-go-lucky, naïve, pagan attitude of the Greek world.

"Personality is a mystery, but at any rate we can attempt to locate it in the order and evolution of the universe.

"What we inherit is not a ready-made affair but a wide possibility and potency of moulding ourselves in our lives.

"There is something more in us over and above this inherited endowment. The freedom must belong to an agent; the plasticity implies a creative moulder. I inherit various capacities, but my own Personality itself is not inherited, but is uniquely and originally mine. I inherit a definite animal body, slightly different from those of my parents and ancestors; I likewise inherit a mental structure, somewhat resembling theirs, but much less so than my body resembles theirs.

"But over and above this organic and psychic inheritance there is an individuality, an individual personality, which makes of this double inheritance a uniquely different blend and composition. The flavour of each human person is uniquely and absolutely individual.

"However similar the inheritance may be, yet I an a new person, a new self-consciousness, a personal centre absolutely distinguished from those who gave birth to me and transmitted their qualities to me. The unique whole, called Personality, is not inherited, however much its constituent qualities and elements have been inherited. And the very character of the inheritance implies a new conscious centre to which they belong, a centre which will organise them freely and creatively into a new unity.

"There is evidently no hereditary character in Personality as such; great Personalities arise from generations of the commonplace; and, again, the great Personality may be followed by generations of the undistinguished.

"Even this great spiritual sport (*as we may call it*) may find its law in the end. But at present it is still utterly individual and incalculable.

"The appearance of Personality, therefore, marks a new departure. It is not merely an addition to the universe but involves on organic transformation of it. On this lofty pedestal psychology and philosophy alike place the personal self or Personality; and surely in this...they are right.

FUNCTIONS AND IDEALS

"As a whole, as the individualising power and activity of Holism, the Personality is fundamentally an organ of self-realization. As in the case of the growing...organism the whole manifests itself by bearing through all obstructions and overcoming all obstacles in its efforts to realise and complete itself or its type in each individual case, so too the Personality has, as its central end, the straightening out of all difficulties and the elimination of all elements which militate against the attainment of its own immanent ideal.

"The food which enters the organism as alien material is destroyed as such in the process of metabolism and is assimilated as blood and other substances and goes to feed the organic system and to form an essential part of it. And similarly the Personality through perception, intuition, conception and emotion, etc., assimilates the influences of its environment and works them up into its own substance—its inner world of thought and will and emotion. And the more thoroughly this mental or personal assimilation is carried out, the richer and more distinctive the Personality is. The wider the range of its acquisitions, the more powerful and thorough the intellectual and emotional assimilation, the more complex and the grander is the Personality.

"Now in proportion as the Personality fails to achieve the character of a perfect whole, in the same proportion it is merely mechanical in its action, and therefore in the same proportion it becomes externally determined or un-free in its actions. The result is that the Personality is partly (*so far as it is a whole*) free, and partly bound or externally determined—that is to say, in so far as it is or behaves like a mechanism. Thus the fuller and more complete a Personality is the greater its power of central self-control, or the fuller its freedom.

"So long as disharmonies exist in the Personality and conflicts arise between different tendencies in it, so long the Personality will fall below its ideal of a pure homogeneous Whole. That ideal will be attained only when in the progress of personal development harmony and internal peace have been secured.

"It must not be supposed that the only manner in which this peace is possible is by the elimination or absorbtion of all the lower or earlier phases of personal evolution and the survival of the later higher phases. The Ideal Man will not be devoid of those passions and emotions which ordinarily war against the higher tendencies and aspirations of the Personality. But in the Ideal Man they will not cause conflict by contending for a dominating position in the Personality.

"Learn to be yourself with perfect honesty, integrity and sincerity; let universal Holism realise its highest in you as a free whole of Personality; and all the rest will be added to you - peace, joy, blessedness, happiness, goodness and all the other prizes of life."

THE HOLISTIC UNIVERSE

"The 'wholeness' or holistic character of Nature appears mostly in this field or environment of Nature, with it friendly intimate influences, and its subtle appeal to all the wholes in Nature, and especially to the spiritual in us. The fact is that the Holism in Nature is very close to us and a real support in all our striving towards betterment. Our aspiration is its inspiration, and it is thus the inner guarantee of eventual victory in spite of all setbacks and defeats.

"There is not only poetic value but profound truth in the spiritual interpretation of Nature to which Wordsworth and other great poets of Nature have accustomed us. And that truth is not merely due to the creative part which mind plays in the shaping and fashioning of Nature. It is not merely that we invest Nature with our own emotional attributes. It is, in fact, to be traced to far deeper sources in our human origins.

"For we are indeed one with Nature; her genetic fibres run through all our being; our physical organs connect us with millions of years of her history; our minds are full of immemorial paths of pre-human experience. Our ear for music, our eye for art carry us back to the early beginnings of animal life on this globe. Press but a button in our brain, and the gaunt spectres of the dim forgotten past rise once more before us; the ghostly dreaded forms of the primeval Fear loom before us and we tremble all over with inexplicable fright. And then again some distant sound, some call of bird or smell of wild plants, or some sunrise or sunset glow in the distant clouds, some mixture of light and shade on the mountains, may suddenly throw an unearthly spell over the spirit, lead it forth from the deep chambers, and set it panting and wondering with inexpressible emotions.

"For the overwrought mind there is no peace like Nature's, for the wounded spirit there is no healing like hers. There are indeed times when human companionship becomes unbearable, and we fly to Nature for that silent sympathy and communion which she alone can give. Some of the deepest emotional experiences of my life have come to me on the many nights I have spent under the open African sky; and I am sure my case has not been singular in this respect. The intimate *rapport* with Nature is one of the most precious things in life. Nature is indeed very close to us; sometimes perhaps closer than hands and feet, of which in truth she is but the extension. The emotional appeal of Nature is tremendous, sometimes almost more than one can bear.

"Nor is it merely we humans, with our intense psychic sensitivity, who feel this appeal of organic or holistic Nature. All organic creatures feel it too. The new science of Ecology is simply a recognition of the fact that all organisms feel the force and moulding effect of their environment as a whole. There is much more in Ecology than merely the striking down of the unfit by way of Natural Selection. There is a much more subtle and far-reaching influence within the special or local fields of Nature than is commonly recognised or suspected. Sensitivity to appropriate fields is not confined to humans, but is shared by animals and plants throughout organic Nature.

"We have seen that the creative intensified Field of Nature, consisting of all physical organic and personal wholes in their close interactions and mutual influences, is itself of an organic or holistic character.

"It is the environment, the Society—vital, friendly, educative, creative—of all wholes and all souls...Without idealising it unduly we yet feel that it is very near and dear to us, and in spite of all antagonisms and troubles we come in the end to feel that this is a friendly universe."

Bibliography

Anon The I Ching (*translated from Chinese by Richard Wilhelm and Cary F. Baynes*). Bollingen. New York. 1950

Aristotle Ethics (*translated from Greek by J.A.K. Thomson*). Allen & Unwin. London. 1953

Benson, Herbert; Miriam Klipper The Relaxation Response. William Morrow. New York. 1975

Berne, Eric Games People Play. Grove Press. New York. 1964

Bolles, Richard Nelson What Color Is Your Parachute? Ten Speed Press. Berkeley. 1970

Boorstin, Daniel J. The Creators. Random House. New York. 1992

Campbell, Joseph The Hero With a Thousand Faces. Princeton University Press. Princeton. 1949

Chopra, Deepak Ageless Body, Timeless Mind. Harmony Books. New York. 1993

Chopra, Deepak Creating Health. Houghton Mifflin. New York. 1987

Confucius The Analects (*translated from Chinese by Simon Leys*). W.W. Norton. New York. 1997

Covey, Stephen R. The 7 Habits of Highly Effective People. Simon & Schuster. New York. 1989

Farr, James N. Experiencing Aliveness. Farr Associates. Greensboro, North Carolina. 1985

Gray, John Men Are From Mars, Women Are From Venus. HarperCollins. New York. 1992

Harris, Thomas A. I'm OK, You're OK. Harper & Row. New York. 1967

Heinlein, Robert A. Stranger In A Strange Land. G. P. Putnam's Sons. New York. 1961

Ni, Hua-Ching The Complete Works of Lao Tzu. Seven Star Communications. Santa Monica, CA. 1979

Ornish, Dean Love & Survival. HarperCollins. New York. 1998

Ornish, Dean Stress, Diet & Your Heart. Henry Holt. New York. 1982

Plato Great Dialogues (*translated from Greek by W.H.D. Rouse*). Mentor. New York. 1956

Redfield, James Celestine Prophecy. Warner Books. New York. 1993

Siegel, Bernie S. Peace, Love and Healing. Harper &
Row. New York. 1989

Smuts, Jan Christiaan Holism and Evolution. Sierra
Sunrise Publishing. Sherman Oaks, CA. 1999

Thorndike, Lynn History of Medieval Europe.
Houghton Mifflin. Cambridge, MA. 1917

Definitions

Whenever you read something, you'll discover this simple truth: if you don't understand the words being used, you don't understand what you read.

To help you gain a clearer understanding of *LifeCycle*, this edition contains definitions of some key words. While words can have several meanings, the following shows the meanings as used in this book.

For expanded definitions, or for words not covered here, feel free to make use of any dictionary which is comfortable for you.

Accession – *n.* an increase by something added. [1580-90; < L ACCESSION]

Adept – *n.* a skilled person; expert. [1655-65; < ML ADEPT(US) one who has achieved skill]

Alzheimer's – *n.* a condition involving increasing loss of mental ability, memory lapses and confusion. [1907; condition described by Alois Alzheimer]

Aspiration – *n.* strong desire or ambition. [1375-1425; < ME < L ASPIRATION]

Avid – *adj.* enthusiastic; dedicated. [1760-70; < L AVID(US)]

Cognitive – *adj.* involving the mental processes of memory, judgement or reasoning. [1580-90; < ML COGNITIV(US)]

Dialogue – *n.* conversation between two or more people. [1175-1225; < ME < OF DIALOGUE < Gk dialogos]

Endeavor – *v.i.* exert oneself to do something; make an effort. [1350-1400; < ME endeveren < IN DEVOIR to make an effort]

Hemlock – *n.* a poisonous drink made from the plant *Conium maculatum.* [before 900; < ME HEMLOK]

Holism – *n.* a natural force which works toward the creation of wholes in the universe, causing wholes to be successful and thrive. [1926; HOL + ISM; word created by J. C. Smuts in *Holism and Evolution*]

Holistic – *adj.* using the concept of holism in theory or practice. [1926; HOL(ISM) + ISTIC]

Intriguing – *n.* that which arouses strong curiosity or interest. [1640-50; < It INTRIG(ARE) < L intricare]

LifeCycle – *n.* a process in which a person takes small steps in all five parts* of their life to achieve what they want most (*healthy body, great relationships, successful career, enjoyable surroundings, peace of mind). [1999; LIFE + CYCLE; word created by S. Holst in *LifeCycle*]

Luminous – *adj.* radiating light; shining. [1400-50; < ME < L LUMINOS(US)]

Meditation – *n.* deep thought or reflection; spiritual introspection. [1175-1225; < L MEDITATION]

Psychical – *adj.* involving the human mind or soul; mental (rather than physical). [1855-60; < Gk PSYCHIK(OS)]

Rapport – *n.* connection, harmonious relationship. [1530-40; < F RAPPORT(ER)]

Synthesis – *n.* bringing together of separate parts; combination. [1580-90; < L < Gk SYNTHESIS]

Tangled bank – *adj, n.* land alongside a river covered with plant growth. [C. Darwin in *Origin of Species*]

Trammels – *n.* hindrance or impediment to free action; restraint. [1325-75; < ME tramayle < MF TRAMAIL three-mesh net < LL tremaculum]

Wholeness – *adj.* complete; containing all the parts. [before 900 < ME HOLE whole < OE hal]

Extra Forms

This is an extra set of the forms presented in this book. You can use these instead of writing in the earlier pages of the book, if you choose.

Or these pages can be given to a friend so they can do the LifeCycle process also.

What Would You Like To Have?

MARK ONES YOU'D LIKE TO HAVE

Health

Good enough to enjoy life	☐
Athletic competitor and winner	☐
Overcome a problem	☐

Money

Have a little more than now	☐
Really wealthy	☐
Need enough for retirement	☐

Relationships

Have more relationships	☐
Get someone really great for you	☐
Solve current relationship problem	☐

Security

Be less worried	☐
Feel much safer	☐
Deal with anxiety, depression	☐

Respect and Appreciation

Want a little more of it	☐
Would like to be famous	☐
Overcome some disrespect	☐

MARK ONES YOU'D LIKE TO HAVE

Success

Want your fair share of it	☐
Reach the very top	☐
Recover from a past problem	☐

Leadership

Enjoy having more people around you	☐
Many people follow the direction you go	☐
Escape a demanding person	☐

Things

Better personal belongings	☐
Beautiful home and property	☐
Replace something that's run-down	☐

Activities

Sports you really enjoy	☐
Vacations to fantastic places	☐
Overcome something that limits you	☐

Friends

People you like to be with	☐
Friends who help make your life better	☐
New, fascinating people interested in you	☐

Take another look at the things you marked above and pick out a few which mean the most to you. Which ones are highest on your list? Which give you the greatest feeling of, "Yes, I want that!" Copy them here, and maybe add some specific details or examples after each.

○ _______________________________________

○ _______________________________________

○ _______________________________________

○ _______________________________________

○ _______________________________________

That's a very good start. Clearly visualizing what you want is the first step to getting it.

Take a minute to re-read the things you wrote on these lines. Imagine how it would feel to have those good things in your life.

Now consider this. Those things are real. Other people have them. You can have them. Soon you'll see how you can bring them into your life.

Where You Are Today

Each line in the following list has two choices. Consider which one has more to do with your life *today* and mark the box next to it. If both choices do not seem highly relevant to you, pick whichever is more relevant than the other.

There is no right or wrong answer on these. Go with your first impression on each of them—that always gives the best results.

Try to pick a box on the left or right each time. Only mark the box in the middle if you really can't say one applies more to your life than the other. Mark one box on each line.

	A	**B**	**C**	
1. You are popular	☐	☐	☐	You are in shape
2. Your things need repair	☐	☐	☐	You are worried
3. You often have organic food	☐	☐	☐	You are a supervisor
4. You are anxious	☐	☐	☐	You are shy
5. You are well-paid	☐	☐	☐	You see much greenery
6. You are tired	☐	☐	☐	You see much graffiti
7. Your things are new	☐	☐	☐	You are relaxed
8. Your things are cheap	☐	☐	☐	You have enemies

	A	**B**	**C**	
9. You are calm	☐	☐	☐	You are invited
10. A glass-ceiling is above you	☐	☐	☐	You are depressed
11. You have bonuses	☐	☐	☐	You have friends
12. You are often concerned	☐	☐	☐	You often use medicine
13. You go to parties	☐	☐	☐	Your things are well-kept
14. You are a loner	☐	☐	☐	You have illnesses
15. You are energetic	☐	☐	☐	Your things are soothing
16. You are underpaid	☐	☐	☐	Your things are dirty
17. You feel reassured	☐	☐	☐	You often use vitamins
18. You often have fast-food	☐	☐	☐	You are supervised
19. Your things are expensive	☐	☐	☐	You get advancement
20. You are solemn	☐	☐	☐	You are overworked

That wasn't so hard, was it? I've been told the choices offered are a little strange, but it does work.

Now, go over the results and see what you get. For example, in the Health group below, "1C" means: if the third box on line 1 (*Box 1C*) has a mark in it, fill in a circle under the Health group. If not, don't fill in a circle. Then go on to Box 3A, and so on.

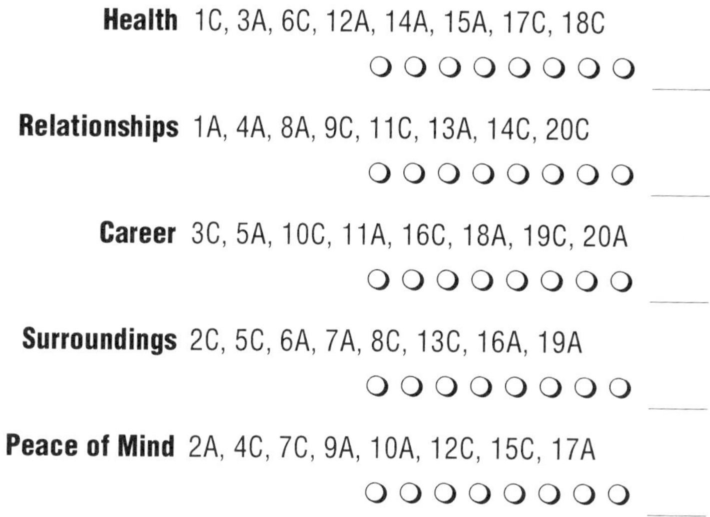

Health   1C, 3A, 6C, 12A, 14A, 15A, 17C, 18C

○ ○ ○ ○ ○ ○ ○ ○ _____

Relationships   1A, 4A, 8A, 9C, 11C, 13A, 14C, 20C

○ ○ ○ ○ ○ ○ ○ ○ _____

Career   3C, 5A, 10C, 11A, 16C, 18A, 19C, 20A

○ ○ ○ ○ ○ ○ ○ ○ _____

Surroundings   2C, 5C, 6A, 7A, 8C, 13C, 16A, 19A

○ ○ ○ ○ ○ ○ ○ ○ _____

Peace of Mind   2A, 4C, 7C, 9A, 10A, 12C, 15C, 17A

○ ○ ○ ○ ○ ○ ○ ○ _____

After you've gone through all of the boxes, count up the number of filled-in circles in each group. Write that number on the line following the circles.

This is what the results mean: the highest numbers are the areas where you seem to have the greatest strengths at this point. The remaining items are where you can make the fastest progress, since they are not yet up with the other areas.

If you happen to end up with all the numbers being about the same (*all are 3-4*) that's actually a good starting place too. It means all the areas are about the same for you, so you can pick any of the five in terms of where to start adding to your life.

Healthy Body Steps

Remember the word you chose in the previous chapter? Think of some small **things** you could acquire which would remind people of that word. For now, just consider things related to having a healthy body. Jot them here.

Examples: related books on that subject, photos, souvenirs, certificates, sports equipment, clothes, posters, tools-of-the-trade, magazines, music, household items, office items, and cards-letters-gifts from others.

Things ___________________________________

you ___________________________________

could ___________________________________

acquire ___________________________________

Now think of some things or activities in your life the way it is today, which suggest the **opposite** of that word. Remember we're just looking at your health and body at this point. Jot those here.

Opposite ___________________________

of ___________________________

your ___________________________

word ___________________________

Next, think of some **skills** you could acquire, or ongoing **activities** you could do—related to having a healthy body—which would remind people of the word you chose. Note those here.

Skills ___________________________

and ___________________________

activities ___________________________

____

For example, if you picked the word **wealthy** you might have come up with thoughts on the three lists which include items like the ones below. Note that these are very small steps that almost anyone could do.

Health   You've been exercising in your garage.
You could get a membership at an upscale
gym. (*Not an expensive, exclusive club
unless you can afford it. Stay within your
means.*)

You don't know which end of a golf club
to hold. You could buy a reasonable set of
clubs, get five relatively inexpensive lessons
and be a week-end golf player.

If for some reason you find you're not really
interested in doing the things you identified, pick
another word that works better for you. The things you
come up with should be relatively easy and things you
could see yourself doing.

Now go over your three lists above:

Acquire: things you might get

Opposite: things you might fix

Activities: things you might do

Add any new thoughts which occur to you.

Next, pick **one** thing from the lists which meets
these criteria: it's something you could do easily and
soon, without too much cost.

Copy that one item here

Health:

Great! Save this step and we'll come back to it.

Great Relationships Steps

Similar to what we did in the previous section, let's consider some things you can do to bring the benefit of great relationships into your life.

Think of some small **things** you could acquire which would remind people of the word you identified earlier. For now, just focus on things related to having good relationships. Jot them here.

> *Examples: related books on that subject, photos, souvenirs, certificates, sports equip-ment, clothes, posters, tools-of-the-trade, magazines, music, household items, office items, and cards-letters-gifts from others.*

Things   ________________________________

you   ________________________________

could   ________________________________

acquire   ________________________________

Now think of some things or activities in your life the way it is today, which suggest the **opposite** of that word. Remember we're only addressing your relationships at this point. Jot those here.

<table>
<tr><td align="right">Opposite</td><td></td></tr>
<tr><td align="right">of</td><td></td></tr>
<tr><td align="right">your</td><td></td></tr>
<tr><td align="right">word</td><td></td></tr>
</table>

Next, think of some **skills** you could acquire, or ongoing **activities** you could do—related to having good relationships—which would remind people of the word you chose. Note those here.

<table>
<tr><td align="right">Skills</td><td></td></tr>
<tr><td align="right">and</td><td></td></tr>
<tr><td align="right">activities</td><td></td></tr>
</table>

To give an example in this area, if you picked the word **wealthy** you might have come up with thoughts on the three lists like these.

Relationships   Jot down the names of some people you know who have wealthy relatives or friends. Invite one of your friends and their well-to-do relative to dinner at a nice restaurant. Enjoy that world for an evening. You may even get an invitation in return.

When you can afford it, do it again with different people.

Now go over your three lists above:

Acquire: things you might get

Opposite: things you might fix

Activities: things you might do

Add any new thoughts which occur to you.

As before, pick **one** thing from the lists which meets these criteria: it's something you could do easily and soon, without too much cost.

Copy that one item here.

Relationships:

Excellent! Save this step and we'll come back to it.

That's real progress. You'll find developing these ideas and steps will become easier each time. On to the next!

Successful Career Steps

Think of some small **things** you could acquire which would remind people of the word you chose earlier. For now, just focus on things related to your career(s). Jot them here.

Things   ___________________________________

you   ___________________________________

could   ___________________________________

acquire   ___________________________________

Now think of some things or activities in your life the way it is today, which suggest the **opposite** of that word. Remember we're only looking at your career at this point. Jot those here.

Opposite   ___________________________________

of   ___________________________________

your   ___________________________________

word   ___________________________________

Next, think of some **skills** you could acquire, or ongoing **activities** you could do—related to having a successful career—which would remind people of the word you chose. Note those here.

Skills

and

activities

____

For example, if you picked the word **wealthy** you might have come up with thoughts on the three lists like these.

Career   Your workplace or office is full of junk. You could clean it and put in some golf things or similar items.

Your clothes are OK but not quite up to others at the office. You could buy one very good outfit and wear it on special occasions.

Now go over your three lists above:

Acquire: things you might get

Opposite: things you might fix

Activities: things you might do

Add any new thoughts which occur to you.

Like you did before, pick **one** thing from the lists which meets these criteria: it's something you could do easily and soon, without too much cost.

Copy that one item here.

Career:

____

Very good! Save this step and we'll come back to it.

In the course of developing these steps you may be surprised by some of the things you come up with. That's good. It shows you're broadening your horizons and expanding your growth opportunities.

Enjoyable Surroundings Steps

Let's identify what you can do to bring the benefits of enjoyable surroundings into your life.

Think of some small **things** you could acquire which would remind people of the word you chose earlier. For now, just look at things related to your surroundings. Jot them here.

Things ______________________________

you ______________________________

could ______________________________

acquire ______________________________

Now think of some things or activities in your life the way it is today, which suggest the **opposite** of that word. Remember we're only addressing your surroundings at this point. Jot those here.

Opposite ______________________________

of ______________________________

your ______________________________

word ______________________________

Next, think of some **skills** you could acquire, or ongoing **activities** you could do—related to having enjoyable surroundings—which would remind people of the word you chose. Note those here.

Skills

and

activities

Using our example of how this might look with the word **wealthy,** you might have come up with thoughts on the three lists like these.

Surroundings   You've still got an old couch in the living room. You could replace it.

You've been going to an average place to get your hair cut or styled. Find someone who's got a great look and start going where they go.

Now go over your three lists above:

Acquire: things you might get

Opposite: things you might fix

Activities: things you might do

Add any new thoughts which occur to you.

As you did earlier, pick **one** thing from the lists which meets these criteria: it's something you could do easily and soon, without too much cost.

Copy that one item here.

Surroundings:
____

All right! Save this step and we'll come back to it.

You're almost done. Just one more to go, then we can start the enjoyable work of bringing these good things into your life.

Peace of Mind Steps

To begin this phase of your journey, consider what you can do to bring benefits from peace of mind into your life.

Think of some small **things** you could acquire which would remind people of the word you chose earlier. For now, just look at things related to relaxation and peace of mind. Jot them here.

Things	_______________________________
you	_______________________________
could	_______________________________
acquire	_______________________________

Now think of some things or activities in your life the way it is today, which suggest the **opposite** of that word. Remember we're only addressing your peace of mind at this point. Jot those here.

Opposite	_______________________________
of	_______________________________
your	_______________________________
word	_______________________________

Next, think of some **skills** you could acquire, or ongoing **activities** you could do—related to having peace of mind—which would remind people of the word you chose. Note those here.

Skills

and

activities

Following up on our example of how this might look with the word **wealthy,** you might have come up with thoughts on the three lists like these.

Peace of Mind   Your vacations tend to be repeated visits to relatives. You could do one trip to Hawaii or Bermuda, and bring back mementos for your home and workplace.

Your work and life tend to be stressful. You could sign up for a weekend stress reduction program at a local spa.

Now go over your three lists above:

Acquire: things you might get

Opposite: things you might fix

Activities: things you might do

Add any new thoughts which occur to you.

As before, pick **one** thing from the lists which meets these criteria: it's something you could do easily and soon, without too much cost.

Copy that one item here.

Peace of Mind:

That's it! Now you have all the things you need to start bringing into your life all the benefits you've identified. Let's go!

Getting Your Life Going

Write your key word here—the one that would make you feel good if you were considered exceptional in this way.

Copy the one item you identified at the end of each of the previous sections—the thing which you could do easily and soon, without too much cost.

		TARGET	DONE	TOLD
Health			☐	☐
Relationships			☐	☐
Career			☐	☐
Surroundings			☐	☐
Peace of mind			☐	☐

Now pick the item from this list which seems to be the easiest, quickest, or least expensive to do. If two are about equal, flip a coin. Pick one and write a "1" in front of it. This is the first step you're going to take to make your life better.

Set a target date for finishing this item. Can you complete it this week? Pick the earliest reasonable date and write it on the "Target" line for that item.

This is the moment your life begins to get better.

Start work on that item no later than today or tomorrow. If your life is important to you, just do it. Even if it's only making telephone calls to get information.

Stay on it until it's done. If you have to put something else off to do this, it's worth it. This is an adventure. The results are hard to describe...you'll experience them soon.

When it's done, check off the "Done" box.

One more step on this item, and it's very important. Show it to someone or tell them about it. It's not bragging. It's something you've done and you're letting a friend know. Friends like to know these things. This step is essential because things you share with others or tell them about become "real." Take my word for it, this makes a difference.

Congratulations! One item done!

Check off the "Told" box and enjoy what you've accomplished. Feels good, doesn't it?

That's one down. The LifeCycle process is well under way. There are more rewards ahead

Pick one of the remaining four items.

Write the number "2" in front of it.

Set a target date for it.

Jump on it and do it.

Tell someone.

Catch your breath and enjoy.

Then do the next one.

Something unusual will start to happen. You'll notice as you do the second and third items that they are beginning to interact. The benefit from one starts to help the others.

After you do the third one, catch your breath, then keep going. You need to finish the last two to get the full effect.

Finished all five? Yes!

You've completed the first *full cycle* of improvement in your life.

That's quite an accomplishment. And you're now in a position to share your accomplishments with others.

Take a few quiet minutes by yourself to consider the small journey you've taken. Think back to how things were before you started the LifeCycle process. Have you gotten any insights? Did the five items you accomplished give you a little more of what you want most in life? Did it touch the different parts of your life, and prepare you to go on and have even more of what you want? How do you feel about it?

It's important to write down your thoughts about what you experienced. This simple act helps you keep the benefits active in your life. It's a success, you really accomplished something. Jot your thoughts here.

Success Story

Mark one: ☐ To encourage other people to make improvements to their lives, this story can be shared with others

☐ Don't share it with others.

Your Name ______________________

Date ______________________

Real-life experiences like yours can be inspirational to other people and help them get the energy to make improvements in their lives. Share your story with them by sending it to me in care of: Sierra Sunrise, 14622 Ventura Blvd., PMB 800, Sherman Oaks, CA 91403.

Index

Notes

Holism and Evolution

If you'd like to peek behind the scenes and learn about the foundation on which the LifeCycle is built, reading **Holism and Evolution** will be an eye-opening experience for you.

It's amazing to discover the holistic approach to life sprang from the work of one man. And was published in a single book in 1926. The person was Jan Christiaan Smuts (*pronounced "smoots"—as in "boots"*) and this is his book. It is here that he created the word "holistic" to describe his concept.

Holism and Evolution is available through book-stores and other retail sources. If you cannot find it there, you can order it on the attached form and have it mailed to you.

Have your own copy of

Holism and Evolution

Or send one to a friend

It's as easy as...

1. Tell us where to send it:

NAME____

ADDRESS ____

CITY_________________________________STATE______ZIP__________

If it's a gift, fill in your name:

It's a gift from _______________________________

2. And send a check or money order for

Book 24.95
Shipping 2.95
____
$ 27.90

California residents add
sales tax for a total of **$29.95**

3. To: Sierra Sunrise Books
14622 Ventura Blvd, PMB 800
Sherman Oaks, CA 91403

(Allow 2-4 weeks for delivery)
(You may copy this order form)

LifeCycle

LifeCycle is available through bookstores and other retail sources. If for any reason you cannot find it there, you can order a copy on the attached form and have it mailed to you.

If there is someone you really care about, give them a copy of this book.

Have your own copy of

LifeCycle

Or send one to a friend

It's as easy as...

1. Tell us where to send it:

NAME

ADDRESS

CITY   STATE   ZIP

If it's a gift, fill in your name:

It's a gift from

2. And send a check or money order for

Book 18.95
Shipping 2.40

$ 21.35

California residents add
sales tax for a total of $22.95

3. To: Sierra Sunrise Books
14622 Ventura Blvd, PMB 800
Sherman Oaks, CA 91403

(Allow 2-4 weeks for delivery)
(You may copy this order form)

LIFECYCLE-1